Jack Harris

Harris Ladies

Jack Harris

Harris Ladies

ISBN/EAN: 9783744640459

Printed in Europe, USA, Canada, Australia, Japan

Cover: Foto ©Andreas Hilbeck / pixelio.de

More available books at **www.hansebooks.com**

✖✖✖✖✖✖✖✖✖✖✖✖✖✖✖✖✖

HARRIS's LIST

O F

Covent-Garden Ladies,

For the Y E A R 1787.

✖✖✖✖✖✖✖✖✖✖✖✖✖✖✖✖✖

[Price 2s. 6d.]

H A R R I S's L I S T

O F

COVENT-GARDEN LADIES:

O R,

MAN OF PLEASURE's

K A L E N D A R,

For the Y E A R 1787.

CONTAINING

The Hiftories and fome curious Anecdotes of the moft celebrated Ladies
now on the Town, or in Keeping, and
alfo of many of their Keepers.

L O N D O N:

Printed for H. RANGER, (formerly at No. 23½
Fleet-Street,) at No. 9, Little Bridges-Street, near
Drury-Lane Play-Houfe.

Where may be had,

The feparate LISTs of many preceding Years.

CONTENTS.

ix)

ERRATA.

In page 67 - fecond line of the motto, for
  turned, read *tumid*.
In page 98—ninth line, for *ftoops*, read, *ftoop'd*.
In page 99—third line, for *hazle dark auburn*,
  read, *hazle eyes, dark,* &c.

---

*Correfpondents are informed that no Letters are
received at the Publifhers, but fuch as come
Poft Paid.*

As a treat to the fair Votary of Love, and a Spur to the wanton Youths, that revell in their soft Embraces, we have taken the Liberty of inserting the following Introduction, which tho' it has once before made its Appearance, must, from its date, be almost forgotten; its genuine merit we flatter ourselves, will serve as an apology for its insertion, and the just remarks which it contains, will gain the approbation of all the Cyprian Choir.

INTRODUCTION.

IN the succession of natural things, their progress, and their decay, individuals seem, like atoms in the sunbeams, of little moment, in the great scale of Providence. The preservation of the species in general appears to ingross the whole scope and attention of nature: she is eternally busy in supplying the place of particulars that fall under the hand of time, and by a kind of

plaftic renown reviving in a blooming
offspring the departed fire ; and if you
trace her through all the various motions
in her wide extent, fhe will be every
where found to tend to one great act of
love. To attempt a fuppreffion of this
almighty impulfe in the human fpecies
would be a tafk as rafh and idle as to bid
the hills touch Heaven. All coerfive
bars, all artificial fences thrown up by
the hand of power, againft this prolific
ardor, this effential act, have hitherto
been in all communities, and will for
ever be overleaped and trampled down.

The mighty call will be obeyed ; and
men and women always rebel againft
fuch weak reftrictions : that generous
frenzy which invigorates the foul is in-
vincible, and muft command. Why
then fuch inceffant clamours againft the
votaries of love ? Why are the infults of
the venal juftice, or of the rough-hewn
muzzy monarch of the night, permitted?
Their number is rather increafed than
leffened by perfecution, which in this as
in cafes of a higher nature, rather con-
tributes to advance than leffen the point
at which it aims. No enthufiafm is fo
ftrong, fo ftimulous, as that of copulation ;

tion ; it brings its warrant from nature's
clofeft cabinet, and bears even the feal
of heaven, " Increafe and multiply ;"
all nature ecchoes to the univerfal man-
date.

If it be a true pofition, that " what-
" ever is is right," why fhad the vic-
tims of this natural propenfity, the vo-
lunteers of Venus, the faireft of creation,
be hunted like outcafts from fociety, be
perpetually griped by the hand of petty
tyranny? Do they not facrifice their
health, their lives, nay their reputations,
at the altars of love and benevolence? Let
the fevereft virtue reflect with me a little ; and that they are of vaft ufe to the
community will be furely allowed.

What villanies do they not prevent?
What plots, what combinations, do they
not diffolve ? Clafped in the arms of
beauty, the factious malcontent forgets
the black workings of his foul. Here
even the mifer feels fome throbbing of
human delight; ftealing himfelf, half
unwilling from his nature, he for a fhort
fpace fmuggles fome fmall benevolence,
and before he departs is prevailed on to
leave his foul behind——a guinea——

What

What a miracle ! Does not this give them
more than common fanction ? What miracle can exceed the opening a mifer's
heart ?

In the fair one's embrace the prodigal
efcapes from the fang of the gamefter;
nor is he laid open to the wiles of the
fharper. With her the youth is taught
the leffon of the mind practifed in genuine tafte, aud learns the native ufe of
things. Here the drunkard drops a
while his fwinifh appetite, and gazes
like a man upon beauty. The lawyer
in the cafe of love forgets his quirks and
equivocation, and is for that fhort fpace
honeft and upright. Covent-Garden, that
aggregate of fweets! that Lethe of the
foul! Behold the merchant ftealing from
bufinefs and the city, under the mafk of
night, to the apartment of his Thais,
where, forgetful of carking cares, no
more remembering the rough fea, the
bold wind, nor the dangers of the long-
expected fhip, his heart expands with
tranfport; the lift of bankrupts remains
unread; and her lovely bofom yields
him the higheft of fublunary blifs. Nor
does the parfon forget thofe walks ; here
even he fometimes vouchfafes to call,

prompted

prompted to be fure by a righteous fpirit, to exhort the fifterhood to focial duties; and fometimes perhaps interlines a pfalm with a vifit.

But thefe are private inftances of the advantages reflected upon a community by the fair followers of the Cyprian queen : thefe advantages are trivial when compared to the public good they occa-fion, though cuftom has embronzed them with the infamous appellation of profti-tutes. Do we not owe to them the peace of families, of cities, nay of kingdoms ? This is a point of light in which they are feldom confidered : It is here that rigor bends its brow, and feverity relaxes its edge. Where they removed, which fate forbid ! by hypocritic power, think how terrible might the confequences be. The reftlefs propagating fpirit, the ftimulating energy implanted in us, will work its way : deprive it of food, will bars, bolts, or authority, protect the honour of the wife, the chaftity of the daughter, or the pious matron's virtue ? This wild frenzy, breaking all reftraint, will bear down decency, relation, kindred, and religion——what domeftic bane ! what warfare of humanity litigation ! blood-

fhed ! inceft !——but I forbear, fancy
trembles to revolve the horrid anarchy,
and the mind declines to dictate.

Say then, ye who have fathers, mo-
thers, fifters, brothers, friends whom ye
love, whom ye efteem, will ye not
ftretch your hand hereafter to protect,
will ye not ceafe to perfecute, the fifterhood, whom, reafon tells ye, ye ought
to defend ? Gratitude will inform you that
ye ought. Why named I gratitude ?
Alas ! I had forgotten that it is an un-
practifed worn-out virtue ; or brutal ri-
gour, difguifed like, and mifcalled, juftice, would be taken off from perfecu-
ting thefe benevolent friends to the publick good, thefe prefervers of general
tranquillity, who lay afide all that hypo-
crify admires, all that fafhion with her
varnifhed glafs reflects as amiable upon
the eye of folly, who facrifice efteem,
rank, and fometimes even life, like the
martyrs of old, in their country's facred
caufe ; yet even notwithftanding do they
fuffer ftripes, imprifonments, and (what
cuftom has entailed upon them) con-
tempt : unjuft proceeding !—

To the glory of the city be it remarked,

ed, that in her bosom have lately sprung
up some public spirits, some whose
hearts teem with grateful remembrance,
some few who feel for the common good,
who see with pity's eye those weak individuals languish under tyrant laws, most
infringed by the makers of them. Such
patriot souls, to the honour of this age,
even now exist, who with manly hearts
have confidered this deplorable cafe, and
opened a retreat for hunted or deferted
beauty. How good, how gracious, how
venerable is such an affembly of keepers,
who never fhut the gates againft harraf-
fed worth, but deal out comfort to the
oppreffed with the hand of liberality!
Why fhould the name of a keeper be
treated with ridicule? Is not their keeping a proof of their beneficence, which is
thereby extended to every rank and fta-
tion?

The lovely nymphs, that fhare in
their bounty, have hearts as large, as
univerfal as their defires; and the whole
race of mankind are the objects of their
warm regard. Like true citizens of life,
they fcatter bleffings with unreftrained
munificence. Neither the dread of want,
nor care of children, checks their rapid
career;

career; their courfe is like the Nile, it
enriches wherever it overflows. Spital-
fields rejoices at their approach; and
the famed magazine in the Hay-market
cheers up at their name. The toyman,
the mercer, the millener, the play, and
opera, nay even the parifh church (fometimes) is gladdened with the chink of
their gold; for, whatever exceptions the
parfon may pretend to make to their
calling, he has none to their purfes; and
for rates, taxes, and repairs, he calls
upon them as well as upon the reft of the
flock.

How many a youth, vigorous and
comely, does not the kept miftref, re-
ferve from jail, nay the gibbet, by fhar-
ing with him the allowance of her keeper! The brawny life-guard-man, the
well-made grenadier, whofe pay being
too narrow, for his foul would otherwife
force him to raife contributions on the
public, is by her protected, and his fi-
nances enlarged.

The generous keeper cannot grudge
the allowance; nay, the good that his
gold produces, thus communicated, will
rather cheer his old heart. He will re-
collect

collect that he is thereby saved the labour
of tilling a soil which requires much cul-
ture, and is yet seldom prolific ; nor will
he begrudge his hire to the labourer, who
might otherwise fall a victim to offended
justice. For the deliverance will he re-
joice ; in thinking that he has saved a
citizen, he will, like an old woman, con-
gratulate himself.

Persist, oh ye hoary seers ! persist in
the cause of keeping ; in that you shew
yourselves friends to charity, virtue, and
the state ; continue to cherish these gifts
of heaven ; still hug to your bosom the
cordial, the reviving warmth communicated by youth and beauty : to the dear
girl whom you shall select, be your
purse-strings never closed ; nor let the
name of prostitute deter you from this
pious resolve. Listen not to unmannerly
prudence, let her not argue you from the
good purpose, for she will sometimes
jostle forwards when passion subsides.
What is there in the idea of prostitution,
to which the greatest characters are not
sometimes subservient ? It is not only in
the purlieus of Covent-Garden that prostitutes are to be found. They flourish
in courts, in senates, in halls of justice,

in.

in fleets and armies; nor is the sacred
porch secure from the approach. Is the
soft, the gentle minion of love, so great
a prostitute, as him who, beneath a scar-
let robe, and the dignity of lordships,
conceals a mind fraught with corruption?
Is not the minister of state who sacrifices
his country's honour to his private interest; the admiral whom venality teaches
to avoid the reflects of an enemy; or the
general, whom gold allures from the
path of conquest, more guilty than her?
These are the real prostitutes that de-
file streams of public virtue, and taint
a nation's glory. On these should justice aim the angry bolt, and vengeance
hurl her fiery dart : nor let the black
gown escape him, who in the pulpit af-
ferts the caufe of religion, which he de-
fcends to make a joke of; who holds
forth in public in defence of every virtue,
and in private is the common encourager
of vice. Thefe are claffes that fhould
bow under the rod of Aftrea.

But to you, ye nymphs, whom elaftic
fpirits prompt to propagate the joys of
foft endearments, to footh the foul with
the Circean cup of pleafure ; to you may
laws and magiftrates be kind ; with you
may

may the ſtateſman, the ſoldier, the par-
ſon, the lawyer, and the merchant ſhare
his treaſure.

But never may that caitiff, called a
ſurgeon, be found within your walls;
guard againſt his approach as you value
life, and its ſupport; avoid with care the
contaminated embrace. Remember ſtill
your keeper; ſooth his lambent flame,
preſerve the tepid wiſh alive. With
wiſe expedients rouſe up faint deſire,
and make him young again. Conſider,
if you ſhould neglect your keeper, your
broad-backed gallant will lack his well-
deſerved ſupply. Keepers are the ſinews
of your trade; may they multiply in
number and in wealth; may they be
always ready and willing to keep the call
as honeſt nature bids: ſo ſhall the public
be invigorated; the cauſe of virtue be
promoted; and the hateful name of Ga-
nymede blotted from the book of me-
mory.

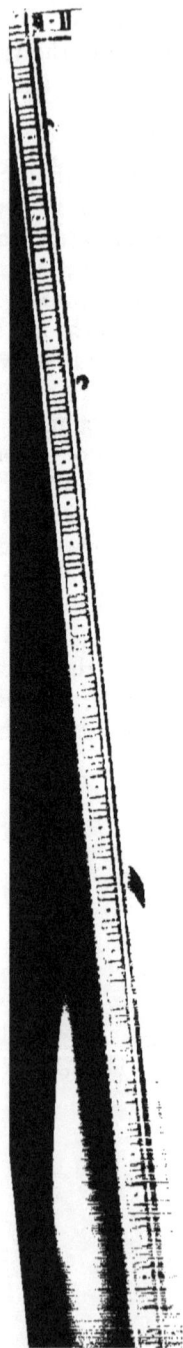

HARRIS's LIST,

OF

COVENT GARDEN LADIES.

Mrs. M—rt—r, of *Covent Garden Theatre.*

Hail love supreme of every joy the source,
That sends to Nature's springs their mighty force;
Expands the soul, awakes the torpid veins,
And gives free force to passion's fiery reins,
And thou dear lust that ope's the miser's heart,
And thro' each callous, each obdurate part,
The thrilling transport guides, be thou my friend,
Let all thy fires with love's soft actions blend,
And then, let times be ever so provoking,
I'll die a *Martyr* to almighty *str—k—ng.*

NO sea born nymph, the Annals of History ever produced, has shewn more love for the sport, or been better

trained in the various arts that ferve to encreafe or prolong the rapturous enjoyment,
than this fweet daughter of the mufes, the
melody of her voice, early initiated her
into the *Beau Monde,* and a fweet enchanting face as early procured her a
train of admirers.

Mr. R—tf—n, a *flender twig* of the
law, would fain in her ftate of virgin
innocence have tyed the Hymeneal
knot, but his diet at that time confifted
too much of the vegetable kind, (at leaft
it is fuppofed fhe thought fo,) to afford
nourifhment fufficient to fupply the defires that Nature at that period feemed
in fo ample a manner to fire her maiden
breaft with, he was therefore only allowed to continue one in her lift of admirers, Captain M—rt—r, the real and
lawful poffeffor of her maiden treafure,
was formed in a different mould; muf-
cular ftrength, nervous activity, joined
to a manly figure gained an eafy entrance
to her heart, and linked in the bands of
Hymen.

Her virgin rofe confentingly was plucked.

Conjugal felicity for fome time fhed
her benignant fweets, o'er the happy
pair

pai: and two prattling cherubs, were the
fruits of their mutual affection, the captain now feemed to be weaning himfelf
from that vigour of affection in proportion, as her wanton defires grew more
extravagant, and from mutual indifference, mutual averfion took place, and
confequently a feparation of beds, which
enabled our Heroine, who was now juft
arrived to that age, when the force of
Nature will not be repelled; when her
defires muft and will be gratified, and
when the glow of love, youth and beauty
had juft reached the Zenith of perfection.
Here then was a feaft for the connoiffeurs
in the art, all the combined forces of
youth, beauty, good-nature, harmony
and fenfibility at once united and refolved upon gratification.

Who was the fecond feafter upon this
world of fweets we are at a lofs to tell,
but poffeffed of fuch a face and form,
fhe could always command her man,
and after fometime had elapfed, in which
it is fuppofed, fhe had traverfed the cyprian market throughout, and was
thereby capable of judging experimen-
tally; fhe attached herfelf to Mr.
W—lde, the Promp—r, and each for
a while feemed happy in each other;

C 2   he

he drew a veil over her *natural* faults, and she in return excufed his natural imperfections, and fought, unmolefted, the means of fupplying the defects; at length Mr. W—d feemed to grow *tame*, and she in return grew more *wild*, and having *heard*, feen, and perhaps *felt* Mr. P—rks *hautboy play*, she made no fcruple of giving the preference where it feemed fo juftly due, but to fhew her former attachment, and knowing his natural fondnefs for a bed-fellow, she actually in form gave him a week's notice to felect a proper perfon to fupply her place, at the expiration of which time she, in a very polite and affectionate manner, took leave, and has fince made Mr. P—ke her favorite man, how long he is to continue fo, is to be proved by the condition and difpofition of his *inftrument*.

Poffeffed of *ten* of Plutus's all-ruling little *deities*, a man of known *parts* may eafily procure her company for a few hours, and *in her* find a moft defirable woman, ftill warm with keen defire, and poffeffed of every fweet enticement to render her paramour burning like herfelf, all animation and tender fenfibility fhall prefs the balmy kifs, with eager grafp entwine the parted limbs, and

and pour the torrent of rapture with all
the fervour of unabated love, and meet
the ſhower of bliſs with all the ardor of
youth untamed and extacy unutterable.

To enumerate the various beauties of
her perſon would require a Thompſon's
thought, or Guido's touch, the moſt
ſtriking feature in which is the eye of
ſparkling hazel, arched by a bow of
the darkeſt brown, and beaming with the
genuine language of her heart, ever
killing, ſave in thoſe tender dye away
moments when they *are wrapt in ſilent
converſe with the ſoul,* and ſeemed drowned in the *coming Elyſium.*

A lively brown ſuffuſes her whole
complexion, and gives additional grace
to every feature, a tender yielding ſmile
ſits preſident, and thro' the pouting balmy
lips two rows of orient pearl diſplay their
magic force : deſcend and view the
lactial hillocks of love, firm as the poliſhed marble, and white as monumental
alabaſter, ſee the *cerulean tubes* ſweetly
branching over the poliſhed ſurface,
and ſhedding their bluſhing influence on
the *roſy ſummit,* diſdaining prop they *ebb
and flow the ſecret wiſhes of the heart,* and
aſk *corporeal preſſure.*

C 3   A *Raven*

A *Raven coloured* furface adorns the
manfion of their *rightful lord,* furrounded
by *beds of never fading lilly,* and raifed
on pillows white as hyperborean fnow.

Mrs. B—nn—r, No. 4, *Walnut-tree*
walk, Lambeth.

I'll find you *war* to fkirmifh every night,
And practice every turn of *amorous* fight :
In *fuch* fweet fingle combats hand to hand,
'Gainft which no woman that is wife will ftand :
My *champion* I'll encounter breaft to breaft,
Tho' I were fure to fall and be o'er preft.

The man may well think himfelf hap-
pier than Paris in the zenith of his voluptuous pleafure, who can encircle in
his arms, and be in full poffeffion of the
charming perfon of this beautiful Helen :
for with the advantage of fuperior height
to moft of her fex, being very tall and
gracefully made ; fhe has a fkin which
would not fuffer the leaft diminution, if
put in comparifon with that of the celebrated dame of antiquity whofe name we
have juft given her. The fimilitude will
hold good in many other refpects ; for,
like her, fhe is of a moft amorous conftitution ;

tution ; like her thoroughly devoted to the Cyprian deity.

Warm as the heart by Cupid newly ſtung,
Sweet as the flower where bees of Hybla hung..

Like her ſhe has an irrefiſtible eye, capable of firing the moſt torpid imagination with as fierce defire, as a torch dipped in the ever-burning flame upon the altar of Venus can kindle, and when once roufed, can raiſe it to that unbearable pitch, that it muſt be quenched in the *bliſsful font* hid within the centre of her bewitching *grove* : Like her too, the pouting lips, rich with more than fancy can expreſs, invite the ardorous kifs, and the panting ſwelling breaſt full of the involuntary ſighs of excefs of pleaſure, folicit the endearing clafp of manly pleaſure, whilſt the titillation of nature in her favourite *ſpot below*, *feelingly* calls for the *Priapian weapon* to receive it in her *ſheath* at its moſt powerful thruſt up to the hilt ; and like her ſhe is perfect miſtreſs of the *ſport*, and can manage any *weight*. An adept herſelf, there is no one fitter to initiate the young officiating *prieſt* in the *deepeſt myſteries* of his *office*.

She

She has fine hair and teeth; at the ripely
lufcious age of twenty-one.

She is not to be had, but at Mrs.
Kelly's, and then only on terms of the
ftrictef honour and fecrecy, having the
happinefs of being at prefent in good
keeping by a merchant of the city.——
Nothing lefs than Bank paper fhe ever
accepts of—indeed we are informed, even
fuch muft be of as many pounds value, as
fhe is years old, fave and except one.

Mifs L—nf—rd, N°. 11, *Glanville-ftreet.*

" Love's power's too great to be with-ftood
" By feeble human flefh and blood:
" 'Twas that which brought upon his knees
" The hect'ring kill-cow Hercules;
" Transform'd his fhaggy lion's fkin
" T' a petticoat, and made it fpin;
" Seiz'd on his club, and made it dwindle
" T' a feeble diftaff and a fpindle:
" 'Twas that made emperors gallants
" To their own fifters and their aunts;
" Set popes and cardinals agog,
" To play with popes at leap-frog."

None

None can difpute the power of love, and none can difpute Mifs L---nf---d's abilities to excite that paffion, or quench it when excited. She is of an agreeable perfon, though not pretty, her hair is dark, and fhe has good eyes, her teeth are white and even, and fhe is of a moft affable temper. She ftrains hard to keep within the bounds of decorum, and makes him who enjoys her imagine he is the only favoured fwain. For this purpofe fhe does not make ufe of the common arts of incitement, nor wifhes to be taken for one of the fifterhood. Her chief rendezvous is in the Green-park, where fhe always walks with a little girl in hand, in order to pafs for a prudent matron; who may have her defires indeed, but is not to be approached with effrontery, or taken by ftorm, but rather with refpect, and feems to furrender to merit only, tho' fhe has the addrefs to get money with her merit.

She has been for fome months (off and on) kept by J— L—, Efq; who has no lefs than three different times conveyed or configned her home to her friends and relations—however all will not do, for fhe is determined not to fubmit to a bare exiftence,

exiſtence, while ſhe can live in gaiety and
pleaſure.

She is tall and genteel, and her age is
not exceeding three and twenty years.

Miſs R—dſh—w, N°. 13, *Margaret-
ſtreet, Cavendiſh-ſquare.*

Although this lady is at preſent in
good keeping, by a certain coal-mer-
chant, her natural amorous inclination,
together with her love of money, entirely
over-balances every duty ſubſervient to a
keeper; with a heart fraught with every
luſcious ſenſibility, ſurcharged with all the
fire of a ſon of Venus by Bacchus, could
be inſpired with, ſhe treads the ample
field of love; nor can ſo lovely a face
be deſtitute of admirers; ſhe meets with
a number, but is rather choice of her favours; no giddy rakes, no flirting fop,
or coxcomb vain, can meet in her embraces; prudence and diſcretion ſhe keeps
conſtantly in view; delicacy and polite-
neſs is her characteriſtic. Her figure is
ſhort, her features conjunctively taken
form what is termed a good face; fine
dark brown hair, dark eyes, and about
one

one and twenty. Fraught with all thefe
perfections, and in all the bloom of womanhood, who can think any fum from
one to three guineas, too much.

This lady was a millener, but that trade
fhe has lately left off, for one more pro-
fitable; however, as fhe loves to do bufinefs privately, Quin's is the houfe fhe
prefers, where you may frequently meet
with her.

Mifs Su——y K——lly, N°. 2, *Princes-
Street, Cavendifh Square.*

My Heart's my own, and fo's my Hand,
  And light and free as air they rove,
No power on Earth fhall one command,
  No mortal e'er preferve my Love.

As fweet variety is not a treafon,
  I'll love to-day, to morrow I'll forget,
And every well-fed fifh that comes in feafon,
  Without controul fhall play within my NET.

No wonder the great fcarcity of money
prevails, when fuch attractions as thefe
are to be found; for that man muft be
                    quite

quite void of sensibility, that would not part with money or life to attain the possession of such charms as these, which is not confined to the meer gratification of a sensual appetite, or the transcient beauties of personal perfection. Her mental charms secure the heart as soon as her personal charms have won it. Her stature is short, but every limb is well proportioned, and just possesses that sweet degree of plumpness that makes a desirable pillow, without being deprived of those abilities that constitute the good bedfellow. She is only eighteen years of age, and but just entered into life. Her face is composed of such sweet, regular features, that united, form a continual smile upon the countenance. Any gentleman having a few guineas more in his pocket than he knows what to do with, and would wish to devote it to the rites of Venus, by visiting the Shakespear, or Rose, they may meet this desirable girl, whose company they never will have the least reason to regret being in, nor will they meet with one whose integrity and honour are more to be depended on.

Miss

Miſs D—nt—t, No 85, *Great Titch-*
field-Street.

This young charmer is about twenty
two with a very pretty face, fair complexion, grey eyes, good teeth, ſhort
and delicate, great animation, indifferent temper, and ſo, ſo, in her behaviour.   She is truly amorous, and ſets
about the rites of love, with her whole
heart ; no diſguſting coyneſs, no for-
bidden frown, no lowering eye, check
her   admirers.   On · the   contrary,
warmth defeats coyneſs, her brows are
ſmooth and placid, and her eyes roll in
the humid fires of tranſports.   She
makes every part contribute its ſhare to
the mutuality of the joy ; and her touch
might as the Poet ſays

———   Kindle frozen appetite
And fire e'en waſted nature with delight.

Though not naturally religious, yet ſhe
concurs iñ one part of the liturgy of the
church of England, namely " to ſtreng-
then ſuch as do *ſtand,* to comfort and
help the *weak,* and to *raiſe up* them that
fall."
    She has lately been in good keeping,
              D   by

by a merchant in the city, whom she
loft by the haftinefs of her temper, having on the conclufion of his laft vifit,
charged the watch with him.

Mrs. N—wl—nd, No. 32, *Goodge*
Street.

The wanton, mighty Jove, in all his glory,
With all the art of elegance divine,
Found the nymph, coy, and blind to all his
    charms ;
Till, chang'd at laft into a golden fhow'r,
The precious drops diffolv'd her into love.

How applicable are thefe lines *to*
Mrs. N——, to whom, not Jove himfelf
would be acceptable without gold, and
limping Vulcan would be tenderly em-
braced, if plentifully ftored with it ; fhe
then can melt into tranfports, and make
the prefent lover believe he is the only
one, for whom fhe has a real regard.
In part, fhe fays true ; fhe *has* a real regard for him, which will continue as
long as his purfe or his liberality lafts;
or until fhe meets with a dupe, more rich
or liberal. Her age is about twenty, her
                    eyes

eyes grey and lively, her complexion
fwarthy, her teeth and beauty middling, her temper agreeable—when fhe
pleafes. There is no afcertaining her
price, it being always as much as fhe
can get ; and her commodity, like
thofe fold by inch of candle, is always
knock'd down to the higheft bidder.
She has not been in life more than two
years, and the name fhe now goes by,
is that of her favorite man.

**Mrs. Mck—z—, No. 12, *John-Street,*
*leading to Portland Street.***

Gods, what a fcene of joy was that ! How faft,
I clafp'd my charmer to my panting breaft !
With what fierce bounds I fprung to meet my
    bl fs,
While my rapt foul flew out in ev'ry kifs,
'Till breathl fs, faint, and foftly funk away,
I all diffolv'd in reeking pleafures lay.
How fweet is the remembrance yet, this night,
Too hafty fled, driv'n on by envious light.

It is very difficult, in a review of
beauties, to avoid a difgufting famenefs
of defcription. Women being com-
D 2 pofed

pofed of face, body and limbs. Eyes, nofe and mouth, being parts of every face, it is almoft impoffible to defcribe different beauties in different terms. What then can be faid of Mrs. M—— that hath not been faid already of other ladies; though indeed, fuch an arrange-ment of feature as her's, is not common. Middle fized, fair and lovely; young and chearful, comprehends all that is poffible to utter, and all belong to her. She is formed to excite defire, and dif-pofed to gratify our wifhes. She adds a poignancy to the tranfient hour, and makes time fly with eagle's wings, when in her company. Her behaviour is na-turally good, and ftudioufly obliging, charms with eafe and delicacy; and even when fhe gives a loofe to love; when fhe raifes the foul to extatic un-defcribable blifs, fhe preferves a con-duct that ever dignifies enjoyment, and deprives it of difguft. Can three gui-neas be too much, for fuch a compa-nion.

She is juft come from the North, as her fpeech will teftify; is faid to be in keeping by a Yorkfhire gentleman, there-fore wifhes to make her other amours as private as poffible. Mrs.

Mrs. P—tt—rf—n, No. 85, *Great Titch-field Street.*

I felt, perfectly felt, what I adore,
Th' enchanting touch give blifs unknown before.
Th' immortal pleafure ran thro' all my frame,
Thro' all my bones and inward marrow came,
That melted and ran down before the impetu-
    ous flame.

This lady is about three and twenty,
has fine light eyes, and hair, alfo good
teeth. She is of a tall genteel ftature,
happily fixed juft above the middle fize.
She is kept by a captain H—y, of the
navy, who conftantly refides with her,
while he is in town; yet fhe admits of
other vifiters in his abfence, more to in-
dulge a paffion for variety, than from
any lucrative views. She is alfo thereby
enabled to form a judgement what age
and difpofition is beft fitted to give joy.
We hear fhe fays, from experience, that
youth gives the *fhorteft*, m turity the
ftrongeft, and age the *longeft* pleafure.
Now, as it is a maxim with her that thofe
joys are moft to be preferred that are of
the *longeft duration*, fhe thence embraces
her old gentleman with the moft ardent
glee, and declares fhe prefers his length-

D 3 ned

ened embrace to the *fire* of maturity, or the *bafly fpur* of youth. Her reafon for her conclufions appear founded on experiment, and her theory is deduced from practice. She argues thus: the eagernefs and impetuofity of *youth* make the tranfports merely momentary. Furnifhed with a profufion of the *coin of love*, they pay the *liquid toll* almoft as foon as they have *entered* the *gate*; nay, fometimes at the very *portal*, without giving time to get their *change* ready, to the difappointment of the turnpike-woman, and the great abridgement of the pleafure of paying and receiving. It is true, they may be able, to make fpeedy repetitions of the *toll*, but then they are all under the fame circumftance, 'till the laft; which in proportion as it approaches the condition of the aged traveller, becomes more fweet, becaufe the more lafting.

The *mature* voyager to the gulf of Venus, has, it is true, a fufficiency of coin, ftays longer in port before he pays his tribute, and, by lengthening the pleafure hath a great advantage over youth, juft as *one* guinea is worth more than *ten* fhillings.

The

The *aged* traveller cannot boaft of repeated payments in a few hours, but his
payment is juft; he has the coin in his
purfe, though it may require more time
to get the ftrings open. He may not be
fo able a mathematician as to *raife* a *per-
pendicular* in an inftant; but, with a little
kind affiftance, it is raifed; and the
time loft in the erecting, is full paid by
the pleafure of proceeding gradually
through every fhade of love, from the
pale rencounter, to the dazzling vivid
ray of the brighteft colour of extacy.
In all this time the *toll gatherer* is approaching, by degrees, to a capacity of
receiving and returning the change. The
value is enhanced by expectation; and,
like a creditor who has waited long for
his due, the payment is received with
double joy. Thus argues Mrs. P—tt—r-
f—n, and the reader is to judge of the
force of her reafoning; but he muft remark, that by *age* fhe does not mean
decripitude, both of which do not fo often
depend on a ftated number of years, as on
the courfe of life. Many love merchants
retain their credit beyond threefcore,
whilft others more prodigal, are abfolute infolvents at thirty.

Mifs

Mifs L—nl—y, No. 11, *Glanvill Street*.

They danc'd around, but 'mongft the reft was feen
A lady of a more majeftick mein;
And as fhe mov'd or turn'd, her motions good,
Her meafures kept. and ftep by ftep purfu'd.
Admir'd, ador'd by all the circling crowd,
For wherefoe'er fhe turn'd her face they bow'd.

This lady was the niece of no higher
a perfonage than a Welch walher woman;
but having a talent for dancing, fhe came
to town with the view of getting upon
the ftage in that quality. She is pretty
in her perfon, of a middle ftature, pleafing, neat figure, dark hair, and chearful temper. She has had many admirers, but a certain *Sergeant*, who was
long a *houfe keeper*, beating up for recruits, fhe inlifted under him, and is now
in his fervice; where, being very expert
in her *exercife*, fhe performs her *evoluti-
ons* to his great fatisfaction. Some indeed fay, fhe is fometimes ab'ent without
furlow, and makes fome excurfions in
foreign fervice; but as fhe has never
been caught tripping, fhe cannot be
efteemed a *deferter*. She is about 21
years of age, and well deferves as many
fhillings for a fingle embrace.

Mifs

Mifs Su—y B—rns, No 11, *New Comp-*
ton Street.

Embrace me clofe, join thy lips to mine,
There's no fecurity in other joys.
Here happinefs is rivetted alone,
Here nothing fades, nothing decays, the fweets
Immortal are, and never ceafe to fpring.

She is a pretty woman, middle fized,
of an agreeable perfon, and chearful temper, about twenty three, with dark eyes
and hair. She feldom goes out *marau-*
ding, but expects private vifiters at home,
where their reception is both genteel
and enticing. She was for fome time
the darling of a certain captain, who
might be a very good paymafter in the
coin of love, though an abfolute infol-
vent in any other money. Indeed, in
refpect to her, he might have let her
have a fufficiency for maintainance,
however he *might get it.* For many have
been known who would be liberal
enough to their miftreffes, though the
brewer and baker went unpaid, and
their wives unclad; fulfilling the lines
of the poet,

For whilft abroad, fo prodigal the dolt is,
Poor fpoufe, at home, as ragged as a colt is.

Though

Though indeed we may acquit the captain of that prodigality as he was never known to be liberal of any thing but—promifes.

Her prefent friend is a Mr. D——ls, to whom fhe is under great obligation, and indeed would be much more fo, were it equally in his power, as it is in his inclination. A guinea is her ufual fee.

———————————

Mifs S——y H—gh—s, No. 40, *Ogk-Street.*

> An age in her embraces paft,
> Would feem a winter's day ;
> Where life and light, with envious hafte,
> Are torn and fnatch'd away.

Were it not that fportfmen look on all kept ladies, as fair game, Mifs Sally would not have a place within this lift; nay, we imagine that whoever purfues her will be thrown out in the chace ; as we, after the moft diligent enquiry, cannot find that fhe has once failed in her fidelity to her friend.

She is now about feventeen years old,
tall

tall and well made, though rather inclinable to fat. Her teeth very even,
her hair dark, and fhe has a lovely pair
of dark eyes. Her behaviour is perfectly confonant with decorum, and her
conduct guided, by prudence. So
formed and accomplifhed, it is no wonder fhe is beloved by her friend, who is
a Shoemaker of opulence in Oxford
Street. Mr. R——s love for her, firft
fixed on her good qualities, and is rivetted by the well founded opinion of
her being entirely his own ; in which he
is the more fecure, from her not being
handfome, but on the contrary much
pitted with the fmall pox; yet fhe retains a good complexion. In fhort, fhe
wants nothing but the facerdotal fiat, to
put her on a complete level with the
moft *legally* virtuous woman.

Mifs Br—wn, No. 5, *Kings Place.*

'Tis juft four years fince this lady was
fit for fervice, and its juft as long fince
fhe has been in actual employment ;
moft of her time has been in the city,
but finding her commodity getting ftale
in

in that market, fhe opened her fhop at a diftant part, where her bufinefs foon increafed ; indeed fhe refufes neither men nor money; and we are told, but we hope without much foundation, that fhe is remarkably fond of the gin bottle, fhe is fat, with light hair, and a pretty fparkling blue eye, her teeth are but indifferent, but the fmell of the juniper takes off every offence that the teeth may occafion, and makes her a *defirable piece*.

Mrs. R—b—nf—n, *Carrington-Street, May Fair*.

Entranc'd they did lie,
'Till Alexis did try,
To recover new breath, that again he might die;
Then often they died, but the more they did
fo,
The nymph died more quick, and the fhepherd
more flow.

This lady is delicate in her complexion, elegant in her figure, and decent in her manner. Her eye, indeed, is not *lively*, but is *languidly charming*, and is what the poet ftiles.

The

The sleepy eye that speaks the melting soul.

In short, on some tender occasions, it seems to be turned inwards to view the soul's content. She is about twenty two years of age, and is now in very good keeping, by C——l G——d.

Early knowing the inconvenience of dependence, she has assiduously avoided any connection with the *mother abbeffes*, and trades entirely on her *own bottom*, in elegant furnished lodgings ; where her price is seldom less then paper, for either a *flying skirmish* or a *whole night's siege*. In her endeavours to please, we are credibly informed, she spares no pains ; and is truly of the *melting mood* ; so that like the skilful gardener, she plentifully showers down the genial dew on whatever seed is sown in her parterre.

She is partial to the private intrigueing houses, where you may be certain of meeting with her, without danger of interruption.

———————————

Miss W——tf—n, No. 11, *Glanville-Street*.

Now let us start and give a loose to love,
Feast every soul, with most luxurious pleasure.

E   This

This is a girl indeed feafts *every* fenfe. Seeing and feeling, are feduoufly employed by her, in proportion. to the price, from five fhillings to two guineas. She is about twenty, rather fhort, but lewd, frolick and gamefome, has a pretty roman nofe, with fine black hair and eyes, and would be more agreeable to many, if fhe drank and fwore lefs. She is an excellent pofture miftrefs, and has ftudied each of *Aretine's* attitudes. She very readily difplays her naked charms, and willingly exhibits *Eve's water gap,* without a fingle *fig-leaf.*

Mrs. Gl—fsf—d, No. 11, *Southampton-Buildings,* *Holbern.*

————To know delight they hafte,
And panting in each other's arms embrac'd ;
Rufh to the confcious bed a mutual freight,
And heedlefs prefs it with their wonted weight ;
The thoughtlefs pair, indulging their defires,
Alternate kindl'd, and then quench'd their fires.

This lady takes her name from a gentleman who is in the fea fervice of the Eaft India Company, and who from
particular

particular attachment left her an allowance of two guineas per week, during
his abfence.

She now diverts herfelf with other fea
officers, to increafe the fum of her pocket money. Her ftatue is tall, her eyes
and hair are dark, and her complexion
rather fwarthy, aged twenty one. As
fhe never takes lefs than a guinea for a
difh of tea, and a game at *tee-to-tum*, it
may be eafily fuppofed that none but
captains can afford to caft anchor in her
port. However, we are affured there is
good *riding*, no *foul ground*, nor any fear
of *firanding the cables*, as fhe admits no
veffel without a *clean bill of health*, and
due examination. Not being willing to
brook difappointment, a favorite Hair-
dreffer is often called to fill up her *vacuum*.

Mifs Efther Sp—nc—r, at No. 31,
Goodge Street.

This lady has carried on, with the help
of a tolerable perfon, a very good trade
for fome years paft. In her earlier days
fhe had a *fafhionable* education ; that is
to fay, fhe has been taught to dance and

E 2   ftudy

study the Graces, &c. but with respect
to any useful instruction, has not the
least knowledge ; but however, not-
withstanding, there is a pretty nothing-
ness in her conversation, which makes
her a very agreeable companion for an
hour or two ; she has but indifferent
teeth, dark hair, a fine forehead, and a
very good leg; is about twenty six years
of age, and though tall and lusty, is
very fond of the blackamoors hops.

Mr. B——, a Confectioner, not far
from Bond Street, is said to be her particular favorite. As to her terms, she
varies according to the circumstances of
the case, just as it may happen.

Mrs. V—n—s, No. 62, *Newman Street*,

Is (we presume) a young widow,
about twenty-one years of age, as she
has lately been at Ostend, and was from
thence conveyed home, by a gentleman
of the city, who has since proved a very
good friend to her.

She is a most elegant and inviting woman ; and, in our opinion, not inferior

rior in point of *beauty*, to any of the
higheſt beauties in his Majeſty's domi-
nions; her face, her air, her gait, appear to be ſomething almoſt more than
mortal ; her perſon is tall and delicate ;
her eyes dark, bright, and ſparkling;
her eye-brows are black as ebony : ſhe
wears her hair dreſſed in a kind of ro-
mantic manner; the treſſes ſeem inter-
voven by the fingers of Love; her neck
is moſt delightfully formed; and her
complexion is finely animated by the
pure tints of Nature, which Art vainly
attempts to imitate : her teeth and lips
are ſo beautiful, that the moment ſhe
opens her mouth, you perceive the
beauty of pearls, and the ſweetneſs of
roſes ; in a word, ſhe is full of graces ;
nothing is more ſoft than her looks,
more pleaſing than her carriage, or more
moving then the ſound of her voice :
an air of gaiety and inexpreſſible tenderneſs breathe around her, but ſo happily tempered, that, though every one
who beholds her muſt admire, yet ſhe
has *knowledge* enough to be prudent, and
takes care to be in a very fair way of
becoming, in a ſhort time, entirely in-
dependent. Her price is five guineas,

and she may be generally met with at Kellys or Westons.

Mrs. W—dg—r, *at a Perfumer's in Rathbone Place,*

Is an unexperienced dame, having just left her friends in Hampshire ; she appears to be a well meaning girl, has natural sense, but by no means cunning enough for her present profession, for we have always found it as true as any axiom in Geometry, that the *Swains* will take as mean advantages of the Nymphs as the latter can of them, which in our opinion, is very much to their disgrace, and needs no argument to prove the truth of the assertion. Poor Nancy is a mere *Je vous remercie Monsieur.* But however, she *must* of course, and by fate and necessity, soon learn better ; she has very fine red hair, remarkably long, and good teeth ; her complexion is particularly fair, and as far as we can judge entirely unassisted by Cosmetics ; she dresses neat, but not at all in the stile of a *fille de joye,* but there is no doubt she will soon *mend,* unless she should

(43)

fhould foon fall into the hands of fome
rational keeper (which we own is a
fcarce animal) who has fenfe enough to
improve her natural good nature and
gratitude, to the improvement of her un-
derftanding and his own felicity.

She has, however, been given to un-
derftand that her favours are of the full
value of two pounds two.

———————————————

Mifs Ll—yd, No. 9, *Bolton Street,*
Piccadilly.

A very fine girl of about feventeen
years of age, has exceeding fine dark
eyes and hair, with teeth like polifhed
marble, but, though fhe excels moft of
the fifterhood in charms, fhe is very inferior to them in feveral other things,
which by fome are thought requifites,
fuch as diffipation, thoughtleffnefs, ignorance, &c. but we think fhe has
fcarcely mirth enough, for fhe has a
white melancholy or leuchocoly, which,
though it feldom laughs or dances, yet
is a good eafy fort of a ftate, and *ca ne
laiffe que de s'amufer :* fhe is very fond of
a cleaver young fellow, efpecially if he
be

be an able *poſture-maſter*, for ſhe is particularly fond of that ſame diſh only
dreſſed in a different manner, as per ex-
ample, *poulet a le broche, poulets enra-
gent, poulets en baches*, poulets en *frica-
ſees* ; kiſſing here, kiſſing there, ſtill
that *ſame thing* in a different manner.
She expeæs two guineas, not having been
in life more than that number of years.

Miſs V—ll—rs, No. 28, *Titchfield Street.*

This lady is very ſingular in her converſation and dreſs, ſhe ſays whatever
comes uppermoſt in her mind, and can
ſing a very good ſong ; as to her dreſs
it is at all times airy and negligent, but
in the ſummer ſhe goes almoſt in a ſtate
of *pure nature,* not conſidering with the
poet, that what is ſaid of wit, may be
applied to beauty. " Beauty is nature
" to advantage *dreſſ'd.*"
The public gardens and play-houſes
are the chief places that ſhe reſorts to,
at all which ſhe is very well known, and
drives on a pretty extenſive *manufaætory*
in her own *garden* ; ſhe is about twenty-
one,

one, red hair'd, and very fair, has good
teeth, and Joves the fport to diftraction,
where there is any thing to be gained ;
for a young fellow of ability in perfon
and pocket will be fure to be *drain'd* to
the utmoft *valuable produce.* Her price
is two guineas, fhe is befriended by a
Mr. W———t, a wealthy citizen.

Mifs Gl—v—r, No. 3, *Glanville Street.*

" But the nymph difdains to pine,
" Who bathes the wound with rofy wine."

Forfaken a few months fince by her
keeper, who was an excellent friend to
her ; but fhe cafts all forrows away in a
bumper, and very wifely confiders only
the prefent hour as worth her care and
confideration : fhe is a Lincolnfhire girl,
about twenty-two years of age, has been
a votary to rapture and mirth about two
years, and finds her prefent beft friends
among the Playhoufe frequenters. She
is a tall genteel looking woman, with
fine blue eyes, light hair, good teeth,
but a violent hot temper'd madam after
all.

Mrs.

Mrs. Wr—g—t, No. 37, *Union Street.*

Immoderate pleasure all her looks express'd,
Unbridl'd transports strove within her breast,
Broke through her eyes, and scorn'd to be suppress'd.

She is tall and genteel, about twenty
eight years old, fair complexion, and
her face very agreeable, her teeth are
good, her hair reddish, and her temper
easy, free and complying. She is
thoroughly qualified to give pleasure,
and is no niggard of her endeavours.
Her touch is delicate, and conveys thrilling sensations; and she is superiorly
eminent for moving a repetition of joy,
by a thousand love provoking actions;
her price is one guinea, but she is far
from being mercenary.

This lady is very lately come from
Gosport, where it is said she had the good
fortune of getting a husband. *Legally,*
however, they soon parted by mutual
consent, and he again took to traversing
the ocean.

Miss

Miss N—wc—mb, *at Mrs. Adams's, King's-Place.*

With thee I'd break thro' laws divine and hu-
    man,
And think them cobwebs, spread for little man,
Which all the bulky herd of nature breaks,
The vigorous young world was ignorant,
Of all restrictions. 'Tis deceit now,
Not more devout, but more decay'd and old.

Restraints of reason, ties of blood,
marriage vows, and prudential maxims,
are all weak barriers, when Miss N—w-
c—mb appears, opens her arms, and ex-
cites to pleasure. Her teeth invites the
burning kiss, her stature tall, but quite
genteel. Her complexion pleases the eye ;
and her soft plump body rebounds from
the close embrace, and demands repeated
pressures. Her yielding limbs, though
beautiful when together, are still more
ravishing when separated. And when
properly placed between them, we may
cry out with the poet Addison,

    , I'm lost in extacy.
How shall I speak the transports of my soul ?
I am so bless'd I fear 'tis all a dream.

Other beauties indeed, may give
                                    equal

equal joys, but few like Mifs N —b can continue them ; others may *forge* chains, and put them on their lovers, but few like her can rivet them. Her great prudence, uncommon with the fifterhood, keep her admirers attached to her ; and none can quit her but with regret. From ftrangers, (who muft be gentlemen) fhe expects a genteel compliment ; but when once acquainted, fhe abates in her demands, in proportion as fhe increafes in her attachment.

She has fine dark eyes, with light brown hair, and is about nineteen years of age. Has not been in trade, more than a twelvemonth.

Mifs R—b—nf—n, No. 9, *Glanville Street.*

When love gives law, beauty the fceptre fways, And, uncompell'd, the happy world obeys.

This lady is fair, well fhaped, fine fize, with lovely black hair, and piercing eyes. She is about twenty two, and hath not been in trade for herfelf above half a year. She is very good tempered, and

and is really a fine piece of temptation. She is faid to be fond of pre-eminence, and loves to be *uppermoft*; fo fhe is thoroughly qualified for the knighthood of the *garter*, as fhe cannot only *tame the dragon* but even *ride St. George*. Her price for either *mounting* or being *mounted* is one pound one.

Mrs. Wh—te, No. 14, *John Street, Portland Street.*

Where love its utmoft vigor doth employ,
Ev'n then 'tis but a reftlefs wand'ring joy;
Nor knows the lover in that wild excefs,
With hands and eyes, what firft he would pof-
    fefs;
But ftrains at all; and, faft'ning where he
    ftrains,
Too clofely preffes with his frantic pains:
With biting kiffes, hurts the twining fair,
Which fhews his joys imperfect, unfincere:
For ftung with inward rage, he flings around,
And ftrives t' avenge the fmart, on that which
    gave the wound.
But love thofe eager bitings does reftrain,
And, mingling pleafure, mollifies the pain.

              F   This

This young lady is formed to fulfil
the obfervations in the motto. She
raifes defires to the utmoft pitch, and
exalts rapture fo high, that it can go no
further, but muft recede. 'Tis true,
indeed, fhe does her utmoft to renew the
pleafure, and generally fucceeds, until
nature is exhaufted and demands time to
refill the emptied cells. She is about
twenty two, fhort and lufty, of an
agreeable countenance, and pleafing in
her manners. She has lately been in
high keeping, by a Major M———o,
but now fhe may be won for two guineas.

Mrs. D—x—n, No. 50, *Newman Street.*

What images fhall eloquence prepare,
To paint a form fo perfect and fo lovely ?
Others by flow degrees advance in love,
And ftep by ftep, and leifurely get ground ;
We article with judgment ere we yield ;
Reafon rejecting oft where fancy's found.
She feizes hearts ; not waiting for confent,
Like fudden death that fnatches unprepar'd ;

Like

Like light'ning's flame, fcarce feen fo foon as
　felt.
All other beauties feem inferior ftars,
At her appearance, vanifhing apace ;
Whene'er fhe mounts, they fet.

This is great praife, you will fay,
gentle reader, but it is truth. She is
truly lovely, truly agreeable both in perfon, conduct, and converfation. She is
of a middling fize, but delicately proportioned ; her hair and eyes are dark,
her teeth fine, her breath like the fragrance of new mown hay ; and fhe is
about twenty four ; yet her external
charms are the leaft of her merit ; her
lively difpofition, and engaging temper,
rife fuperior to them, and confirm her
conquefts. She is not to be approached
by audacity or indelicacy, for any money ; but the man of addrefs, and ten-
dernefs, may be admitted to a partici-
pation of her charms for three guineas.
In the light, though cheerful, fhe is
rather referved ; but at night fhe ful-
fils the expreffion of Sciolto.

When blufhing from the light and public eyes,
To the kind covert of the night fhe flies ;

　　　　　　　　With

With *equal fire* to meet her lover, *moves*,
Within his arms, and, with a *loose* she loves.

She sings excellently, and can play on
the Guittar very prettily ; by birth we
learn she is an American, but is lately
come from Scotland. Her particular
friend is a Captain M———, but he
does not altogether engage her.

Miss Charl—tte C—ll—ns, *Oxford*
Buildings, Oxford Street.

The loaded kine about the cottage stand,
Inviting with known sound, the milker's hand.

Charlotte is about three and twenty,
her hair is black, her teeth indifferent,
her breasts round and small, her stature
under sized, but her arms and legs are
too much in the gothic stile. She was
bred a dairy maid in Staffordshire, but
an ensign in a marching regiment, took
her from *milking* the *cow*, and taught her
to *stroke* the *bull*. She soon after was
quitted by him, and the stage waggon
brought her to town. On her arrival
she hired herself to a cow-keeper near
Islington.

Iflington. Thus fhe kept her hand in, till being feen by a Bridewell Boy, who married her and put her in lodgings, where befides *milking* him; fhe fometimes employs her leifure hours, in handling other teats, and is faid to have not only a delicate hand at *ftroaking*, but great fkill in the ufe of the *churn*, foon making love's *butter* from nature's cream. She is fo very agreeable, and fo well accomplifhed in that branch of the dairy, that had fhe cunning, equal to her other qualifications, fhe might greatly encreafe her profit; but fhe is void of art, and always takes what is given to her, be it either gold or filver. However, that is a fault that will mend with time; and when fhe is taught to fet a proper value on herfelf, fhe will be more fought than at prefent.

Dear variety would not let her be long conftant to her youthful hufband, for fhe foon fupplied his place in the perfon of Dick P——— the Bayliff's fon.

Mifs

Miſs G—l—w—y, at No. 9, *Glanville Street.*

Beauty to no complexion is confined,
'Tis of all colours, and by none defin'd.

This is a ſhort, fat, fair complexioned, good natured girl; very lively and very complying; ſhe deſerves cuſtom, for ſhe is ready to oblige her cuſtomers, any way they chuſe, and will take what they pleaſe to give, never haggling for price. This, ſometimes, is to her advantage; for truſting to a gentleman's generoſity, ſhe frequently gets more than ſhe would have preſumed to aſk. At other times indeed, ſhe meets with diſappointments, for there are ſome ſo very mean as, when their *pipe* is out, to refuſe paying for the tobacco.

She has only been four months in trade, is about twenty years of age, has light hair and blue eyes, her teeth are rather large, but good, and ſhe has been very genteely brought up.

Mrs.

Mrs, Cl—l—nd, No. 64, *Swallow Str.*

What founds appear, where e'er I turn my eyes,
> All around
> Enchanted ground,
And soft elisiums rise :
> Flow'ry mountains,
> Mossy fountains,
> Shady woods,
> Christal floods,
With wild variety surprize.

When Addison wrote these lines, he little thought he was describing Mrs. Cl—l—nd's *low countries*. Yet the description is just. Soon as the vail is withdrawn, and the traveller has passed *holland*, he is *surprized* with the wild variety he beholds, and is ravished, like the old jewish legislator on mount Pisgah, with a view of the *promised land*, flowing with milk and honey. Her *fountain*, whence flows the impending flood, (sometime like *chrystal*, and sometimes like amber) is edged with delicate *moss*. The *wood* is *shady* and *tufted* ; and the *mountain*, at the top, is not always destitute of *flowers*. Letting the eye wander over the downs from the summit of
> the

the mountain : it firſt beholds, a central cup, with a pretty little boſs in the
midſt ; anu beyond that, on the ſides
of a milk white valley, are two large
white hillocks, with tops of a reddiſh
brown, furniſhed with a great number
of ſmall pipes, for the conveyance of
milk. The reſervoirs of *honey* (which
compleat this lovely *Canaan*) are placed
at a diſtance under the *grove*, and between the moſſy ſkirts of the fountain;
they empty by a number of canals into
the grand avenue ; and will diſcharge
their contents on the gentle friction of a
warm conduit pipe. This honey is as
ſweet to the *feel,* as that of Hybla to
the taſte, and when felt, truly makes
ſoft elyſiums riſe. Many travellers have
viſited this delightful country, and felt
the *honey,* but, only by permiſſion of
the fair lady of the manor, who expects
a fee of two guineas for the licence.

She is a Scotch laſs of about two and
twenty, middle ſized, very genteel, has
good teeth, with dark hair and eyes,
and remarkable pretty arch'd eye brows.

Miſs

Mifs Sm—th, No. 9, *Glanville Street.*

The lovely girl lay panting in my arms,
And all fhe faid and did was full of charms.

Fair, tall, very genteel and agreeable, good complexion, white teeth and about eighteen. Can a girl thus formed fail to pleafe? When good temper is added fhe muft be charming—fo indeed fhe is ; would fhe drink lefs, fhe would have no fault, but it is not fo much for the love of liquor, but purely out of good nature, for the good of the houfe, into which fhe takes her Strephons. This makes her acceptable to the taverns and bagnios ; and with her, you are always fure of a good room, genteel treatment, and diligent attendance ; her price is one guinea.

She is lately come from Yorkfhire, and has not been in her prefent line of life more than feven months.

Mifs Afhm—r—, No. 3, *Poland Street,*
Oxford Street.

All breathlefs they disjoin'd—he backwards drew
The fhrunk machine, from that fweet coral mouth

Whofe

Whofe precious tafte her thirfly *lips* well knew,
Whereon they furfeit, yet complain of drought;
He with her plenty prefs'd, fhe craving ftill,
Revives the *dead* again—again to *kill.*

 This tall, genteel, full grown nymph,
is a very defirable bedfellow for the
warm fportfman in the *Cyprian games*;
here he may purfue the *burning chace*, and
traverfe the *rifing grounds*, the *pleafant
valleys*, and *tufted groves* fo richly *planted*
and appropriated to the votaries of Venus, with as much freedom as the amorous fun kiffes and plays his melting
beams upon every part of the genial
earth, and emulate his warmth as fervently as he pleafes, riot in charms, till
every *fenfe* is filled with *maddening tranfport*, and the fierce anguifh of almoft
unbearable pleafure call for the gratifying
that *fenfe* which, like Aaron's ferpent,
fwallows up the reft, and collecting
every ray of fire, is rendered fo impetuous as to remove every weak barrier
with hot impatience, and force at once
into the *magic circle* of all her charms
concentered, till *ftung* with the *delightful
friction*, her whole frame is bufy to improve and heighten the *killing joy*; hands,
lips, eyes, breafts, all confpire to haften

ten the *blifsful death*, which, being *in*
at, he *enjoys* with unfpeakable pleafure,
whilft the *ftreams* of *fruition pour* on both
fides from every *fp ing* of life, and *min-*
gle all its *fweets* ; breathlefs they lie,
diffolved in extacy, till recovering *life*,
they *pant* again for *death*. She has fair
hair, blue eyes, about twenty years of
age, good teeth, and as fine a pair of
legs as the eye can behold, or the hand
of luxury would wifh to feparate ; two
guineas is her ufual price.

Mifs K—ng, No. 17, *Union Street*.

Every way formed for *giving* and *re-*
ceiving pleafure, fhe *is* a fund of delight
which many a man would be happy to
poffefs, though but for a night. She is
of a dark complexion, well made, and
has a pair of dark blue eyes, which at
every tell-tale glance difcovers the wanton wifhes fo predominant in her foul,
and invite the *blind coral beaded boy* into
her *cloifter* of *teeming joys*, where fhe will
entertain him with as much fpirit and
activity; as moft of her fifterhood; fo
lavifh indeed is fhe, that fhe cares not
how

how much she *spends* upon him, nor will she be at all frugal with refpect to her *guest*, for she cares not how much she drains him of *his liquid* treafure, but will be content with *one piece* of the *folid.*

She has not been above a twelve month in life, is about twenty one years of age, of a good fize, good teeth, and a re-markable fine leg; was lately what is called a fervant maid—at Knightfbridge.

Mifs Y—ng, No. 44, *Berwick Street.*

" I am as willing to *grapple*, as he was to *board.*"

This firft-rate *Frigate* of *Venus* is not afraid of any *man* of war; if she once gets *yard* arm and *yard* arm, she is fure to *engage* with the utmoft fpirit, and let his weight of *metal* be ever fo great, she will lower his *main yard*, and make him *ftrike* to her. She has a very capacious *hold*, fo that if she finds a prize *deeply la-den*, she will *take it all in* with pleafure. She is a very handfome, well built, tight little veffel, but to drop metaphor, (guefling that all my readers are not nautically verfed,) this pretty agreeable

lafs

lafs, has a pair of the moſt expreſſive blue eyes, that ever ſhot the lightning of deſire to the impreſſible heart, and her beautiful auburn locks are well adapted for the toying fingers of the playful amorofo. She has good teeth, which well underſtand the *pleaſing* bite ; has a plumpneſs very alluring to thoſe who love to *feel* what they *claſp*, and in this liking, ſhe is not outdone by any, for ſhe loves to *claſp* the mighty *engine* of the wanton boy in its utmoſt *tumidity*, and to *feel* the *fulneſs* of its *force ſpend* itſelf *within her*, which ſhe never fails of warmly *ſaluting*, and meeting it with a whole *liquid broadſide.* Her diſpoſition is ſo good, that her *antagoniſt* is always ſure to be treated after the engagement in the kindeſt manner.

She expects a brace of golden pictures at or before parting.

Mrs. F—t, N°. 80, *Queen Ann-ſtreet, Eaſt.*

" Subtle *ſenſation* darting through the brain,
" *Die* of a roſe in aromatic *pain.*"

What can a heart fraught with the glowing warmth of luxuriant ſenſibility,

G   and

and fired with an imagination fervent as
the day's bright luminary, which Nature
has impreffed with colourings all her
own, wifh for more than the *full enjoyment* of a nymph young, beautiful, and
lovely in her difpofition, as well as perfon ; *teeming* with fweets, and fwelling
with defire too exuberant, too poignantly
fierce to brook confinement. Nothing
furely can equal the exquifite delight
of *corporeal enjoyments*, heightened by the
delicious imagery of two bufy, lively
creative fancy's, where *foul* feems to
meet *foul*, and *incorporate* with each
other ; *one ftrong painfully fweet* idea
actuating them both, and correfponding
with the two lines above, of our harmo-
nious mafter of melodious numbers,
whilft the groffer fenfes are connected in
the fame band of mutual pleafure ; *rivetted* by every *feeling*, and *giving* and
receiving unutterable tranfports. .

" *Bodies mingling*, fexes *blending*,
" Who fhall moft be *loft* contending."

Such are the delights of this blooming
girl, this living model of exulting nature muft give to the man of rich defire,
replete with the *full breathings* of voluptuous

tuous fancy, and *highly amourous feelings.*
To deſcribe her perſon as it deſerves, requires the pen of the author of the ſub-
lime and beautiful, and the pencil of a
Reynolds; however, we will juſt attempt
a minute deſcription. She is of an elegant figure, and very tall; ſtands on the
temptingly inviting verge of twenty-one,
a very handſome perſon, a fair and good
complexion, dark eyes and hair, white
and even teeth, and has lately been
abroad.

We underſtand ſhe was born in Ireland, and is frequently to be met with
at M.s. Kelly's. Can a piece of fine
Bank Paper be too much for ſuch a
companion? At any rate, ſuch are her
expectations.

Miſs M—rr—s, N°. 81, *Queen Ann-
ſtreet, Eaſt.*

So fond of *love's game,* you never can tame
  The ſpirit inceſſant deſire,
Stirs up in her frame, and blows into a flame,
  You may damp, but not put out the fire.

This lady is tall and genteel, very fair
and delicate, with dark hair and eyes, good
G 2 teeth

teeth and very ſhewey appearance ; a face
which might be called pretty, and of ſuch
an age, that ſhe might with great truth
apply to herſelf the ſong,

" Time has not thinned my flowing hair,"

being only twenty-three. She is not at
preſent in keeping, but has met with a
ſlip incidental to the *ſports of Nature*, having had a child by a gentleman of her
preſent name, who has now left her
to the foſtering hand of a generous public; the ſportſmen of which, will find her
good *game*, and though very *mettleſome*,
eaſily run down. She is very fond of
getting under *cover*, where, if the *terrier*
is a good one, ſhe will ſhew excellent
ſport, the enjoyment of which, is well
worth a couple of ſpare pieces.

Miſs P—ct—n, Nº. 16, *Union-ſtreet.*

O love be moderate, allay thy extaſy,
In meaſure *rain* thy joy, ſcant this exceſs,
I *feel* too much thy bleſſing, make it leſs
For fear I ſurfeit.————

Elegance and beauty mark this engaging nymph for their own ;————with
the

the face of Hebe, and the complexion of a *Ninon le Enclos*, the eyes of an Eloise, and the gracefulness of the deity she is so warm a votary of. She is of a majestic height, has very good teeth, remarkably even, and is at the prime age of twenty-one, glowing with all the fire of youth and love, and with all the exuberance of boiling health, as *full of juice* as the ripe cherry, when tempting the taste by its vivid distention, and of vigor as the goddess Diana in the heat of the chace, she asks that " *full toned* virility that speaks so *feelingly home* to the female heart." She either keeps, or is kept by a certain limb of the law; however, there is a linen draper, whom she is very fond of, as she always finds a *measure* to answer his *yard*; her temper is tolerably good whilst solely under the influence of Venus; but when once Bacchus interferes his potent sway, it becomes very indifferent; however, by the addition of a third deity (Plutus) and giving her one or two of his all-powerful pieces, her brow will be rendered placid, and she may be kept in a very *desirable* mood. She is. remarked for great cleanliness in her person.

G 3   Miss

Miſs H—mm—nd, Nº. 5, *Glanville ſtreet.*

Oh ! let me wander all unſeen,
Beneath the *ſanction* of her *mein ;*
As *velvet* ſoft, as *lillies* fair,
As *honey* ſweet, as diamonds rare ;
There pluck the choiceſt *flowers* of *bliſs,*
And kiſſing *die,* and *dying* kiſs.

It has been ſaid this lady is kept by a
Mr. C— of the city, but we are fully ſa-
tisfied that is not really the caſe, as ſhe is
never denied to any gentleman that aſks
in a polite manner for her ; and moſt will
find her, when they become *familiarly* acquainted, a piece not unworthy their notice. She has a pretty inviting countenance, fair hair, fine blue eyes, and a complexion thatdraws a pleaſing line between
the brunette and the fair, and blends
both in ſuch a manner, as to make a very
pleaſing medium. Her lovely *half globes*
of nature, are nevertheleſs of the faireſt
hue, and ſo *proud* of their ſituation, that
they never ſink below their deſtined
mark ; but though they never fall, they
often elevate themſelves in a very pleaſing
manner, and tell the gazer in very plain
terms, the ſituation of *Cupid's cole hole,*
whoſe

whofe *embers* are now fufficiently warmed, to admit the *red-beaded torch*, which, when buried in her *forge*, fhe can at one fingle *ftroke* mechanically melt down, without much lofs of weight, to a very great lofs of fubftance; and is fo *handy*, that with the greateft facility, in general, fhe can make him recover his former figure. Her lodging is filled with her own furniture, fo that if you would wifh to *lay in* any of yours, fhe expects a guinea a night for houfe-room.

She is allowed to be a very agreeable companion, perfectly fober and well-behaved; aged about eighteen, and of the middle fize.

Mifs Afhf—d, N°. 30, *Goodge-ftreet.*

And as fhe fits in raptures on his knee,
Her hand drew out the *turned monftrous wight*;
Alarm'd fhe *faw*, but wifhing not to *fre*,
She op'd her legs --and *put bim* out of fight.

This lady is very defirous of pleafing all her admirers; and if wanton looks, if amorous well-preffed kiffes, if the mutual intercourfe of the filent language of
tongues,

tongues, can roufe the *dormant fenfe*, you will not complain of any deficiency in that point. If that will not anfwer, fhe prefents you in a fingular manner with a new language of the eyes, and obliges you to falute her heaving, panting breafts: if all thefe attempts prove vain, fhe fcruples not to expofe to public view her *choiceft treafure*, at the fame time demanding a return of the compliment, which when complied with, fhe finds no difficult tafk to *revivify*; fecuring herfelf thus far, fhe never wifhes to lofe time, but inftantly begins the *game*, which fhe then has in her own *hand*, and takes care he fhall not play, fo as to win a *trick*. She is rather tall, and very well made, dark eyes and good teeth, a dark complexion, which fhe improves by the affiftance of rouge; is in her nineteenth year, and wifhes to fee a guinea the firft thing in the morning.

She has only been about a twelvemonth in trade.

Mifs W—lf—n, No. 8. *Blenheim-fteps.*

This tall fine lively girl, has a fair complexion,

complexion, good teeth, light eyes and hair, exceedingly well bred, and promifes to make as good a fportfwoman as any in the *Park*; fhe manages all her *paces* with judgment, and though fhe prefers a *flying leap*, fhe never yet was foiled at a *flanding one*; fhe never wifhes to ufe a *fpur*, neither does fhe chufe *riding* in *boots*, and let the road be ever fo *ftony*, fhe does not regard it, but in general mends her *pace*. Her pleafing countenance wears a continual fmile, and her fine flaxen hair adds a grace to every feature; and although fo lately initiated into the *trading* line, (only five months) fhe never fails examing her *flanding* acquaintance; for as fhe never had the *fmall-pox*, fhe does not wifh to be *inoculated*. Her price, is what you pleafe above a guinea.

Mifs Polly And—rf—n, Nº. 11, *Pittftreet, Charlotte ftreet.*

Torches are made to light, jewels to wear,
Dainties to tafte, frefh beauty, for love's ufe;
Herb for their fmell, and fappy plants to bear;
Things kept unnotic'd are but love's abufe.

Come

Come here and revel then in rich delight,
Feaſt on her charms, and *ſpend* in bliſs the night.

Should a man, whoſe paſſions are fired
with the generous glow of luxuriant ſenſibility, and whoſe fancy is ever preg-
nant with the rich ſtreamlets of humanity
—ſhould ſuch a man, whoſe heart is ever
open to the moſt delightful *feelings* of his
nature, be led by the wayward hand of
chance, or prompted by the irreſiſtible
ardor of inclination to the arms of this
lovely fair, he will find in the deſectable
embrace, every reciprocal joy that can
wind two ſouls to extaſy. For at the warm
inviting age of twenty, with the fluſh of
beauty on her cheek, the complexion of
a Helen, (being uncommonly pretty) the
graceful ſtature of a Juno, and eyes the
colour of the heavenly blue-eyed maid,
—like them too, penetrating, and ſweetly
affable, (with the additional tenderneſs
and amorous ſportiveneſs of the playful
queen of Cyprian pleaſure, they beam
unutterable ſoftneſs upon the fond enraptured gazer) dark hair, good teeth, and
the diſpoſition of a Hebe, ſhe cannot fail
of pleaſing the man of *ſenſible* ſenſuality,
whoſe ſenſibility is ſo finely interwoven
in his temper and conſtitution as to thrill
with

with the moſt poignant ſenſation at the
ſlighteſt touch of the little all-ruling deity,
and vibrate with the pulſation of the moſt
pungent rapture. But as the neceſſities
of life cannot be ſupplied in a vulgar
unharmonized world, without the coali-
tion of Plutus with Cupid, a ſprig of the
root of all evil is abſolutely neceſſary.

She ſings and dances delightfully, and
is in good keeping.

Miſs Betſey M—ll—r, Nº. 30, *Goodge-
 ſtreet.*

Her glances could create a day in cells,
And kindle freezing hermits into dalliance.

She is well made, and rather tall, but
clever and genteel. Her hair is black,
her face agreeable, her features regular,
and her cheeks roſy, as (perhaps) art can
make them. She has tolerable teeth, her
diſpoſition is free, and her temper haſty
Her age is about twenty-two, and for any
one who does not think her too much of
a woman for him, may be a very deſirable companion. Her conſtant place of
walking is in Oxford-ſtreet, where ſhe
may

may be diftinguifhed from other *Ladies*,
by a remarkable large black feather in
her hat. Her price is one guinea—that
is, if fhe can get no more, for fhe is
of that turn, that fhe never thinks fhe has
enough of love or money.

Mifs G———n, N°. 43, *King-ftreet,*
St. Ann's.

" When you meet with one that's froward,
" Saucy, jilting, and untoward,
" Should you act the whining coward,
" 'Tis to mend her ne'er a whit.
" ———Let her, let her go, ne'er mind her."

Middling fized, well fhaped, fair complexioned, light eyes, red haired, quite
pretty and agreeable at firft fight, and
about twenty-three years old. With thefe
qualifications would not one think Mifs
G———n a defirable woman ? But behold the reverfe of this beautiful medal.
Her temper is execrable, and her behaviour fcandalous, fo as to limit the pleafure of her company to the few minutes
employed in enjoyment, and not a moment, either before or after, to any
but

but thofe who are funk in brutal
lafcivioufnefs. Lufcious difcourfe may
be pleafing, but it muft not be *fulfome*;
pleafure may admit of having its lamp
lighted by the hand of luxury, but ab-
hors to have it drowned with ftinking
oil. This lovely, capricious, and difgufting female, will exact from you all
fhe can, previous to enjoyment, after
which its two to one, but fhe abufes you,
for not having ftill more to give her. We
are credibly informed this has been her
practice more than once on different per-
fons.

Mifs B—llf—rd, N°. 11, *Glanville-ftreet*.

Hither hafte while youth invites,
   Obey kind Cupid's prefent voice ;
Fill ev'ry fenfe with foft delights,
   And give thy foul a loofe to joys :
Let millions of repeated blifes prove---
That thou all kindnefs art---and I all love.

This charming girl, were it not for
being rather fhort, might truly be called
the mafter-piece of Nature ; for though
below the ftandard of Mars, fhe is fo

H   com-

compleatly formed to that of Venus, as
to be a delicious morfel for thofe who
delight to *erect* their *ftandard* in a foft
and flowery field, where humid kindly
dews are ever ready to fhed their fweets
on the manly adventurer, who boldly
pufhes on in the amorous combat, till
panting breathlefs in the fierce alarm, no
longer able to fuftain the conflict, he
chufes rather to die in the gap, and
fpend his laft breath in the fervice of the
Cyprian Queen, than to withdraw his
weapon from that fervice, while it has
one fpark of metal remaining from hilt to
point. Her perfon is what we call pretty,
and her age in its moft improved ftate,
for fhe is but eighteen, capable of giving
the matureft joys, with all the zeft of virgin ripenefs, when firft gratifying the
eager tafte, and with all the fpirit and
vivacity of youth; fhe has a pair of
femi-globes, beautifully full, with elafticity rebounding to the tendereft preffure,
and fo warm, that without the help of
natural electricity they would fet a world
on fire, efpecially when added to the
lightnings which flafh from a pair of the
fineft blue eyes that ever fet as deftructive
engines in a female head; but which,
when

when foftened by the imaginary or real
tranfport, glance the mildeft beams, and
fwim in a redundancy of native-fhining
fluid. She is of a dark complexion, with
fine dark hair, which, when unfhackled
by the fetters of art, floats in wavy ringlets, down a pair of well-formed fhoulders; her teeth are good, and her temper no one ever yet found fault with, as
it is perfectly fweet and complying; fhe
was about three months ago, decoyed by
an elderly gentleman into her prefent way
of life, which however fhe prefers to her
former, and does not refufe any vifitant
who is able to cover his approaches to her
covered work with one pound one.

Mifs Betfey Gr—n, N°. 44, *Mortimer-
ftreet, Cavendifh-fquare.*

Now fierce defire does all his mind employ,
And ardent paffion fpeaks approaching joy:
Such is the nature of the pleafing fmart,
Whofe burning drops diftil upon the heart;
The fever of the foul, fleet from the fair,
And the cold ague of fucceeding care.

H 2 This

This girl, although not handſome, is little, lively and wanton, and loves to join Bacchus and Venus together. She is the daughter of a jeweller in the city; and is a very good judge of *precious ſtones*. She likes them beſt indeed, when *rough* and *uncut*; and loves to ſet them in a black *hair* ring. She is very fond of a good ſprig of *coral*, and cares not how *red* the tip is. Though ſhe prefers the kind which the naturaliſts call *ſucculent*; and however hard it may be when put into her hand, ſhe poſſeſſes the natural chemiſtry of making it *ſoft* and flabby. This operation ſhe performs for one guinea, and has good buſineſs. She is about twenty-two, and can make the longeſt hour ſeem ſhort, altho' ſhe has been but one year in buſineſs for herſelf. She ſeldom takes any one home, always pretending to be but a viſitor at the above addreſs.

Miſs M—nſt—n, Nº. 80, *Queen-Ann-ſtreet, Eaſt*.

O what a rapture did my frame ſurround,
When firſt I claſp'd her body cloſe to mine!
'Twas more than rapture all, 'twas all divine.'

Such

Such joys I knew, as words want power to tell ;
Joys, which the feeble reach of thought excell.
My foul furpriz'd at that excefs of joy,
(Still ever pleafing, and could never cloy)
Unable to fuftain it, wing'd away,
Whilft all intranc'd and extacy'd I lay.

This lovely fountain of tranfport is tall
and fair, melting and generous, with light
hair, and light and fparkling eyes. She
indeed knows her value, and expects no
lefs than three guineas and a fupper ; for
fhe is averfe to fhort fkirmifhes, and nothing but a whole night's engagement
will pleafe her. She was born in Edin-
burgh, and was daughter to a bookfeller,
who married her at fixteen to a young
printer ; as he perceived, though very
young, fhe was *ready* for the *prefs*, and
wanted fome one to open the *leaves* of
her *duodecimo*. Her mother alfo was of
opinion, that fhe had better *fmart* than *itch*.
But whether her hufband did not make a
proper *impreffion* ; or whether fhe thought
him too religious, and whilft he conftantly
faid a long *grace* before *meat*, and as long
a *thankfgiving* after every delicious *meal*
'till his food grew cold ; fhe left him
about twelve months fince, and came up

H 3

to London with a young officer. But he
was foon appointed to another regiment,
through na:onal intereft, and left Mog-
gy to fhift for herfelf. She knew fhe was
lovely; and felt fhe was loving ; and tho'
fhe had quitted the printer's *balls* and *frif-
ket*, fhe had no doubt but fhe fhould find
as good. She had faved fome money, had
good cloaths, and made a refpectable
appearance. She affumed the name fhe
now bears, was noticed by fome men of
confequence, and has now fufficient employment.

Mifs Polly Sm—th, No. 12, *Little-Port-
land-ftreet, Soho.*

Bleffings when cheap, or certain, we defpife,
From fure poffeffion what defire can rife ?
Love, like ambition, dies as 'tis enjoy'd
  y doubt provok'd, by certainty deftroy'd.

Convinced of the truth of this maxim,
Polly refolves, if the bleffings fhe difpenfes are *certain*, at leaft they fhall not
be *cheap*. Her demands always rifes in
proportion to the feeming height of defire in her lover. From indifference fhe
will accept of a fingle guinea ; but from
eagernefs,

eagerneſs, and heated imagination, ſhe
will (if ſhe can) exact five. She is truly
worth money, ſhe knows it, and is prudent enough to know, that the harveſt
of pleaſure cannot laſt long ; and the
time will come, when the gold-finches
will fly paſt her ground, and none but
boobies, noddies, and old carrion crows,
will neſtle in her buſh. Thence ſhe
gets all ſhe can, and keeps what ſhe gets ;
and though but juſt turned of nineteen,
has already got the appellation of *ſtingy
Polly*, from her leſs prudent ſiſterhood.
She is a very lovely girl, dark haired, fine
teeth, dark complexion, a good tall
figure, agreeable converſation, and perfectly amiable.

Miſs W—nt---r, No. 17, *Union-ſtreet.*

" Forbidding me to follow ſhe invites me ;
" This is the mould of which I made the ſex,
" I gave them but one tongue to ſay us nay,
" And two kind eyes to grant."

Here we can preſent our reader with
as ſweet a man's woman as ever the
bountiful hand of Nature formed. A
pair

pair of fine dark eyes that dart refiftlefs
fire, that fpeak a language frozen hearts
might thaw, and ftand as a fweet index
to the foul; a pair of fweet pouting lips
that demand the burning kifs, and never
receives it without paying with intereft;
a complexion that would charm the eye of
an anchorite ; a fkin fmooth as monumental alabafter, and white as Alpian
fnow, and hair, that fo beautifully contraft the fkin, that nought but nature can
equal. Defcend a little lower and behold the femi fnow-balls,

" Studded with rofe buds, and ftreak'd with
" celeftial blue ;"

That want not the fupport of ftays;
whofe truly elaftic ftate never fuffers the
preffure, however fevere, to remain, but
boldly recovers its tempting fmoothnefs.
Next take a view of Nature centrally;
no folding lappel, no gaping orifice, no
horrid gulph is here, but the loving lips
tenderly kifs each other, and fhelter from
cold a fmall but eafily ftretch'd paffage,
whofe depth none but the blind boy has
liberty to fathom: between the tempting
lips the coral headed tip ftands centinel,
fheltered by a raven-coloured bufh, and
for

for one guinea conducts his well-erected
friend safe into port.

Miss D—lt—n, No. 14, *John Street,*
Oxford Street.

Pleasure wantons in thy arms,
And revels o'er thy num'rous charms ;
O'er thy cheeks of rosey bloom ;
O'er thy lips that breathe perfume ;
O'er thine eyes so sweetly bright,
Darting soft expressive light.

This agreeable votary of Venus is just
in the genial age for ripened joy, being
about one and twenty, with a person

Fair as the snow-drop of young spring,
And blooming as June's brightest rose.

She has a pair of fine grey eyes, which
dart with irresistible softness, the effusions
of a fancy exquisitely turned to every
amorous sensation, and express such a
height of feeling in the wishful look as
can only be felt by an inamorato as
full of love-fraught sensibility as herself.
Her teeth are good ; she has light hair ;
and her breasts may defy the nicest pen
to

to paint their beautiful proportion, or unconquerable elafticity, with fuch a whitenefs as even modefty herfelf would blufh to look at. She is of a moderate ftature, not too ungainly tall, nor yet too low ; and her temper. feems to be a remarkably good one. A favourite gentleman vifits her, whom it is imagined fhe keeps from the emoluments of her other vifitors. The regions of the Elyfian Bower are well tufted with the fringe of Nature, and no fportfman will think a guinea an object for the liberty of fporting in *fuch* a manor, and difcharging his piece in fo delectable a fpot.

Mifs W—nd—m, No. 40, *Queen Ann-ftreet, Eaft.*

Her pouting lips do breathe ambrofial fweets,
And fweeteft balm diftil when yours it meets:
Her fwelling breafts lie open to the gale,
And teach the lily whitenefs in the vale ;
On Venus' mount the wanton graces fkip,
And cull luxuriant fweets from either lip.

This lufcious looking lafs formerly acted as lady's maid in a very creditable family, but that wonderful reflecting
mirror

mirror, the looking-glafs, the *nofce te ipfum* with the women, was every morning and evening very bufy in painting to our charmer the value of thofe perfonal qualifications *Nature* had fo lavifhly beftowed upon her. This mother of all *things* had likewife been very bufy with the *mother of all faints*, and night-working Fancy, dictated with fuch power and energy the grand ufe of that then *hot-bed of Nature*, that fhe did not want a fecond invitation from the rofy butler to tafte the wonderful Tree of Life. This trade was carried on in fo publick a manner, that it foon reached the ears of her miftrefs, who gave her warning, and prefented to the world a fweet complexioned girl, with blue fpeaking eyes; fine teeth; pouting lips, that are always particularly employed on certain occafions, juft leaving room for the velvet tip to dart its magic influence, and increafe if poffible the raptures the Tree of Life fheds in the moft fertile field of blifs. Her temper and difpofition correfpond with her perfonal perfections, and her abilities under cover exceed, if poffible both,

She

She is about twenty-three years of age—her ſtature is tall, and ſhe may be really called a fine woman; after which it is almoſt needleſs to remark that ſhe cannot but be deſerving a handſome compliment.

Miſs Ch——s, No. 16, *Union Street.*

Fatally fair ſhe is, and in her ſmiles
The Graces, little Love's, and young Deſires inhabit,
And all that gaze upon them are undone.

This is certainly a faſt, and the charms of Betſey are enough to undo any man; neither is ſhe leſs ſkilled in the art of *doing* than in that of *undoing*; ſhe does her ſupine exerciſe with the greateſt judgment, fond of cloſe attacks, always preferring buſh-fighting to any other, and not one of her comrades in the whole corps is more exaſt in firing a volley, or renews their charge with more agility; her piece is adapted to any ramrod; ſhe can enlarge it if too ſmall, and with more dexterity reduce the ſize if too large; ſhe has fine light brown hair, ſparkling blue eyes, a beautiful neck, which ſhe
takes

takes no fmall pains in expofing, a good
complexion, which fhe does not feem to
be indebted to art for at all ; her temper
and difpofition are fluctuating ; if her
man pleafes her, fhe generally contrives
to pleafe him, and if one guinea could
keep her in a good humour, no perfon,
furely would refufe it.
Her age is about twenty-five.

Mifs C—rr, No. 4, *Union Street.*

Oft will fhe cry,
Oh cruel! fye!
Oft weeping fay, forbear :
Oft fhall her hand
Your —— command,
And put it you know where.

This true emblem of lufcious love
has not trod the common path above
two twelve months. A young gentleman of good fortune bore away the lovely
prize from *Norwich,* and, after revelling
in luxurious luft for three months, left
the dejected fair to depend for fupport
on what Dame Fortune fhould throw in
her way. Bleffed with a fweet difpofition, armed with an irrefiftible eye, that
is fhaded by as beautiful a bow as Iris
I ever

'ever formed; good teeth and rofy complexion, bordered by the delicate whitenefs of a lily; remarkably good tempered, and juft paft the twenty firft fummer, fhe cannot fail meeting with a number of admirers, which hitherto fhe has been very choice of, preferring pleafure to profit; at the fame time not entirely throwing afide the latter. She expects two guineas, if only a fingle one, fhe is happy to pocket the affr)nt.

Mrs. B—nf—n, *alias* L—ve, No. 3, *Goodge Street.*

What, Madam, never fober? Jamais, Jamais, Jamais!---Damme.

This lady, with 'a very affected Frenchified refinement and delicacy, is continually by her actions contradicting what fhe would fain be thought, by proving herfelf to be a very Bacchant, unfit even for Comus's train, as fhe is almoft continually in a ftate of intoxication, and will run any length, and fubmit to any thing rather than be deprived of the *good creature*; in her moments of inebriety

briety she talks as long as she *can*, and her whole difcourfe is to fhew the *noble, fentiments*, and refined education she is puffeffed of. She is about two and twenty, of a fair complexion, full breafted, light hair, blue eyes, and good teeth. She is in ftatue, fhort and fat, and rather fond of low company.

Mrs. Br—wn, No. 3, *Princes Street, Leicefter Fields.*

——— Oh ! fhe is
The lovely chance work mafter piece of Nature,
That blufh'd to fee what her own hands had done
As if, miftaking moulds, fhe, unconcern'd,
Had caft ——— in a form divine.

If thefe lines ever were applicable to a human being, Mrs. B——— can certainly lay claim to them. She was *un-virgined* at Norwich by an officer, who foon after was called away on duty, and nought but the great metropolis could then fuffice this beautiful piece of untutored innocence. To defcribe her whole perfon as it prefents itfelf bids defiance to the moft unbounded ftretch of the moft fertile fancy ;

I 2   And

And if imagination fails beneath the pleafing tafk,
Ah ! what fhall language do ? Ah ! how find words
Ting'd with fo many colours ?

No bloom but Nature's ever deck'd her
cheek—a bloom that Art, dreffed in its
moft finifhed ftate, might blufh to look
at—blended with lilies which Nature
calls her own. Her forehead bears the
exacteft medium ; and, influenced by
her temper, never knows a wrinkle, But
no feature feems fo expreffible as her
eye, fparkling in a pool of living chry-
ftal, which never afks a fecond glance to
fecure the heart of a frozen anchorite ;
where the defire of pleafing is fo luxuri-
oufly ftamped that even anticipation is
a heaven : but the look, the touch, the
fweet refifting touch, the inviting fwelling part of the breafts, foon calls for the
gratification of fome other fenfe, in the
execution of which, on her part, fhe has
fome peculiarities. No fooner is the
fwelling engine introduced to quench the
amorous fire, but her wanton tricks begin, and fhe will, if poffible, keep him
in that well formed ftate for two hours ;
fond of *dying*, yet never wifhing for *death*.
The twining of limbs, and the filent
language of the tongue, is never forgot ;
and although fhe is fo well fkilled in the
art of prolonging pleafure, the impetuous

fier

fire of youth, brought to fuch an extacy-
by the antitafte of her perfonal charms,
often very quickly diffolve, and difap-
point the amourous fair ; but if difappointed ftill fhe is not foiled. If manual friction from a hand of lilied foftnefs; if burning kiffes, imprinted by lips
fraught with nectarious balm, and the
moft alluring foftnefs; if the fragrance
of a breath, fweet as fucking infancy,
if all thefe united can reanimate the fallen
victim, frefh life muft foon follow. Thus
are you obliged to fpend the whole night
in amourous rapture. *Somnus* and *Venus*
never met together on her couch: and
fo noble is her difpofition, fo generous
her heart, and fo truly free her mind,
that money is the leaft of her thoughts,
and fhe has been often known to refufe
when her circumftances ftrongly de-
manded the acceptance.

Mifs R—fs—ll, No. 1, *Glanville Street*.

Shall woman, form'd to mould the heart at will,
Degrade herfelf below the beftial herd ;
Or fo with words diftort her outward form
That ev'ry glance, fudden as nitrous blaze,
Shall hatred ftamp, and kill the name of woman ?

We are forry to fay that the ill temper of
this

this lady in a degree juftifies the above motto, being affixed to her character. Neverthelefs, if fuch a pair of femi globes that paint maturity in its fulleft bloffoms; if fuch a fkin as would make the night-born fnow blufh; if fuch a bloom as would bid the damafk rofe look pale, united with the activity and fprightlinefs of two and twenty, can afford pleafure; if well-formed limbs, if a port fo nobly armed as would bid defiance to any attack, and though its antagonift ftands ftiff and true to its point, is fure to make him with mutual fatisfaction fhrink from it; if all thefe charms combined can ferve for temporary enjoyment here you are fure to meet it; but hufh! no more, let every charm filently awake the fenfe; and pray, my fweet loquacious girl, be mute; my fair amazonian beauty, be ftill; nor let thofe martial arms fo often unrivet that affection your perfonal charms are fure to gain. Whilft her temper remains undifturbed by the too volatile effects of the grape, fhe might with fome degree of propriety be ftiled a good-natured girl. A fingle fire through the bufhes half a guinea will purchafe, but a twelve hours encounter under cover will amount to double the
fum.

fum. She is tall and lufty, has good
teeth, with a pair of fine blue eyes.

Mrs. Fr—d—r—ck, N°. 20, *Carlifle-
ftreet, Soho.*

Now quick defire hath caught her yielding prey,
  And, glutton like, fhe *feeds* yet never *filleth* ;
Her lips are conquerors ; his lips obey,
  Paying what ranfom the *infulter* willeth ;
Whofe vulture thought doth pitch the prize fo
    high,
That fhe will draw his ———*rich treafure dry.*

As we are to have a commercial treaty
with France, it may not be wondered at,
fhould we alfo have too great a partiality
for French manners and fafhions, which
the lady in queftion too much affects,
but whether in compliment to her own
country, or that of her profeffed admirers,
we cannot tell ; baring this frippery,
fhe is an agreeable companion for a
fportive night, and will play her *part*
very well, when once heartily *engaged* ;
fhe feeds like a glutton on the *delicious
morfel,* and when the *vivid tube* is rendered *inanimate,* fhe never fails to *animate*
it again with new life and vigor : if the
burning breath of *unfateddefire,* the coo-
ing

ing murmers and foul thrilling kifs can
do it. She is tall in ftature, very genteel,
fine light hair and eyes, good teeth, and
in the prime of life, fome where near
about, tho' not exceeding thirty. She
is a very fhowey woman, and is rather remarkable in having a fine Roman nofe.
A brace of King's pictures is her ufual
expectancy ; but fhe cares not whether
they are French or Englifh, or one of
each of their majefty's fo they are but golden ones.

Mifs C—rt—s, No. 81, *Queen Ann
Street, Eaft.*

What pleafes one man will not fo another,
This fancies one lafs, and that's fond of t'other.

Something or other attracting is always fure to be found in every Woman
of Pleafure : in fome it is the fparkling
fire, or the liquid gleam of the love
fpeaking eye, in fome the bewitching
fmile, or the pouting richnefs of the
dimpled lip ; in fome, the whitenefs of
a bofom, fhort breathing with delight,
or the inviting foftnefs of Nature's femi-
globes ; whilft in others, it is the wanton

ton treffes of their fine flowing hair, curling in amorous ringlets around their necks; or to be more voluptuous, the luxuriancy of the *grove* beneath, and the redundant growth of hair which fo agreeably adorn and defend the pleafing *Mount of Venus* from the rude fhocks of impetuous invafion, and which twining round the *ruby portals* of *Cupid's grotto*, forms a delightful bed for the *root* of the *tree of life*, or the tempting invigorating *feel* of a foft, plump, fwelling thigh. Which of thefe attractions draws this lady her admirers, we cannot pretend to fay; but this we are certain of, that it cannot be all of them united. She is rather fhort, rather agreeable, and rather good-natured — when pleafed; about twenty-two years of age, of a fair complexion, dark eyes, good teeth, and not in keeping, but lived lately with a Mr. D——, of the Temple; fhe fings, and is a very agreeable converfation-piece when fhe pleafes. Whoever has a fuperfluous three or four guineas in his pocket, and is difpofed to lay them out here, will meet a very cordial reception. N. B. She keeps the houfe.

Mrs. Sm—th, No. 16, *Union Street.*

O deeper lust than bottomlefs conceit
Can comprehend in ftill imagination;
Drunken defire muft vomit his receit,
E'er he can fee his own abomination.

Whoever has an appetite to a piece of
fenfuality, as fenfual as his heart can
wifh, let him repair to this Lady's ftandard, in the attick ftory. For any other
charms than that of perfon, fhe has no
pretenfions to, being of a very indifferent temper, infolent, and lewd to a
degree; infomuch that her common
converfation is difgufting to any man of
the leaft refinement in his pleafures.
She has a fair complexion, long nofe,
middling aged, and the fmall pox has
left a number of unpleafing dells in a
face otherwife not a very agreeable one.
Her eyes and hair are rather light, and
fhe has good teeth. Her propenfity to
the fport is fuch as to induce her to be
moft wantonly inconftant, for on any
terms fhe will run all lengths, minding
no rifque to get a frefh morfel of *raw
flefh*, which fhe devours with the greedi-
nefs of a glutton. Her price is juft
whatever you choofe to prefent her with.
Mrs.

Mrs. M—rſh—ll, at Mrs. St—pl—t—n's,
Margaret Street, Cavendiſh Square.

Ye votaries of Venus hither come ;
Come ye voluptuous to this bliſsful Feaſt ;
Here taſte the ſwelling bowl of poignant joy ;
Here crown your revels, here your wiſhes crown ;
Here quench your amorous flame in Pleaſure's lap,
Unbind her Cæſtus, and diſſolve in Love.

This truly agreeable girl has every
charm that can feaſt the ſenſe of the niceſt voluptuary, and warm an anchorite
with deſires which Nature never meant
to paſs ungratified ; her countenance is
beautifully open and engaging, expreſ-
ſively featured, and a bloom ſurpaſſing
every thing but what is beſtowed by Nature on the choiceſt amongſt the faireſt of
creation, beyond the livelieſt tints which
unfold their beauties to the ſun of all her
vegetable tribe ; and above, far above
the delicate ſtrokes of a Guido, the glowing colouring of a Titian, or the breathing ſoul-ſpeaking language of a Thompſon. Her ſtature is above mediocrity,
being tall and luſty, but ſo finely formed
and well proportioned, that every limb,
taken either ſeparately or together, diſplay a ſymmetry equalled by few ; ſo
that

that all true votaries, would do well to
vilit this living Venus, warm with the
genial current of vigorous health, and
rich with the generous. vitality of full
blown youth, only twenty-two, to prefs
her balmy lip, where nectar ever hangs,
to gratify the tafte of thirft itfelf; to
mix their eager limbs with hers, and
catch the burning glow of amorous feeling, in all the twinings of luxuriant love
—till fired by the maddening tranfport
of unutterable fenfation—they haften to
the joy : then her fpreading thighs divide to receive the *tumid guefl*, and prefent to his exquifite touch two lovely
pouting *portals*, which tenderly meet,
and feem to kifs each other, and unite to
keep out the cold, and fhelter the delicate ftructure of the internal part of the
manfion from injury—But at the powerful touch of this welcome vifitant, they
unfold as to their rightful lord, and in-
veft him with all the powers belonging
to the place, which *fhower* down all its
treafures.   After being *entered* fometime
into the *Cyprian cabinet*, in the *fanctum
fanctorum* of the building, the delight
this occafions, can only be *felt*, as no
language can defcribe fuch extafy.

For

—————For who can paint like Nature.

The *grove* however round it, we *can*
fpeak of, is one of the beft ever fported
in by :he *Wanton Boy*, and the *mofs-
crowned mount above*, might well be cal-
fed *Mount Pleafant*, an excellent *Field* to
Graze Inn, which your *nag* might have
the liberty of grazing in a whole night
for two guineas. She has fine dark eyes
and hair, very good teeth, and a fine
complexion.

Mifs M—rfh—ll, No. 44, *Mortimer
Street, Cavendifh Square.*

Here native elegance was made to dwell,
With Beauty feated in her rofy lap,
Mingling their fweets with fuch a tafteful hand,
That full-blown art grows pallid at the fight,
Such then her parts expofed—her *hidden gifts*
Claim juft pre-eminence—fince void of thefe
Superior fenfe ungratified remains.

This blooming actrefs, whofe beauty
and elegance fo juftly correfpond with
her tafte, has been initiated on the ftage
of Love only nine months, her hiftory
we are not fully acquainted with, but

K   from

from the knowledge we have of her present connections, we imagine she must have received a genteel education. Some little time back she was to be met with at almost every public place of entertainment, and was indeed, a fort of fixture at a noted house of intrigue in Margaret Street, at this time, she never stoops below the polite man, or the man of fashion : amongst her then numerous votaries, Mr. H—y seemed to shew her the greatest partiality, nor did her affection from him seem less ; he grew at length tired of her, and we presume she of him. She is an excellent good companion, although of rather a hot temper ; singing appears her delight, in which she does not want ability ; but in her offerings of love she indulges her wanton appetite to its utmost scope, nor *feels* fatiety fo foon as many of the sisterhood : her willing paramour will ever find her arms open to receive the repeated embrace, and whilst he retains the power of giving pleasure, she is sure to possess the same in return.

Pressing with burning lips the quick return,
Or, with enraptured folds fresh bliss invite.

Her

Her perfon and figure is remarkably
elegant, a good complexion, and lively
hazie dark auburn hair, good teeth, and
but nineteen years of age. If you have
two or three guineas to fpare you may
be always fure of a moft ʒgreeable companion in this lady.

———————

Mifs T—pp, No. 31, *Tottenham Street,*
Tottenham Court Road.

——Each female faint he does advife,
With groans, and hum's, and ha's, and gog- ⎫
  gling eyes,   ⎬
To rub him down, and make the fpirit rife : ⎭
While, with his zeal tranfported, from the
  ground
He mounts, and fanctifies the fifter's round,

This demure lady is a conftant fre-
quenter of the Tabernacle, though not
entered into the *fociety.* Her perfon is
charming, her garb plain and modeft,
her carriage exemplary, and her converfation religioufly rapturous. Yet fhe is
never averfe to aflift the brethren to
humble the *lufts of the flefh,* and for a
guinea, will enable any of the congre-
gation

gation to go home quite *cool*. Experience hath taught her the evil confequences of congregating with finners;
thence fhe took the laudable refolution
of miniftering to the wants of the *faints*;
to fome of t'.: preachers of whom fhe
is faid to have lent her *pulpit*, in which
they have thewn themfelves *laborious*
men, who could *melt* her, and penetrate
into the interior receffes of her flefhy Tabernacle; lifting up the *veil* thereof, and
inducing devout raptures. There is indeed one advantage in a connection with
Mifs T—pp, that it is fure to be kept
fecret; and it is only from fome of her
lovers, who have broken from the fociety of the faithful, that we have learned
thefe particulars. She is in the practice
(occafionally) of a mantua maker, is rather of a low ftatue, very pretty and
quite agreeable, has fine dark hair and
eyes, good teeth, and in about her nineteenth year.

The two Mifs Ed——d's, N°. 16.
Union Street.

Treat a woman young in age, and not
old

old in fin, as a *felon*, her fenfe of fhame
will foon be extinguifhed; fhe will be
tempted to look upon herfelf as the out-
caft of fociety, fhe will continue to fin
without controul; her heart will be pe-
trified, fhe will grow indifferent to all
events, caring not how foon, or in
what manner, fhe leaves a world where
fhe finds fo little mercy, and fuch unre-
lenting feverity againft her.

We know the above obfervation to be
fully verified in thefe two fifters, who were,
by the iron hand of Misfortune, forced,
in a manner, to commence proftitutes,
when they were mild, fober, and honeft ;
but having been feveral times feized by
the Noƈturnal Guardians, and as often
delivered over to durance vile, by the
daily *diftributors of Juftice* ; they are become the very reverfe of what they once
were.

Mifs B—ch---m, No. 7, *London-ftreet,*
Middlefex Hofpital.

Here now is a blooming piece in only
her eighteenth year ; fhe has received a
good education, having lately come from
a boarding-

a boarding-fchool, and fhews herfelf quite
the accomplifhed, well-bred girl, of a
fweet, affable difpofition, and one whofe
manners and converfation make her an
excellent companion, and has procured
her many valuable acquaintance : inde-
pendent of her converfible abilities, we
are informed her proficiency in the trade
of love is not lefs commendable, and
ever wifhing to preferve the honour of
the female flag untarnifhed, fhe never
takes a *thing* in *hand*, let her *undertaking*
be ever fo great, but her antagonift is
fure to *fhrink* from his purpofe ; but her
amicable difpofition is fuch, and fhe is
fo confcious of her abilities as a counfellor, that unlefs fhe is fee'd with a fum
fuperior to four pounds, although fhe
wifhes the *caufe* to be pleaded in court
a fecond time, fhe will not fuffer it to
be brought on till the fee is paid.

Her keeper is a gentleman refident in
Berner-ftreet, and we are credibly informed, he was the means of introducing
her into life, not above fix months fince,
by recommending a fudden elopement
from her boarding-fchool ; which, fhe
was not much averfe to.

She is tall, genteel, and very pretty,
with dark hair and eyes.

Mifs

Miſs G—rd—n, Nº. 4, *Union Street,,
near the Middleſex Hoſpital.*

Is the ſacrifice made fit,.
Puſh him forward to the pit,.
Puſh the ſtanding victim on,
And when the noble deed is done;.
Draw the bull of Venus out,
And ſtroke him up for t'other bout..

This ſprightly prieſteſs of Venus has
been initiated but a ſhort time in the
myſteries of the Goddeſs ;, we judge her
to be about eighteen, of a fair complexion, rather ſlim, light brown hair and
eye-brows, which are remarkably fine,
with ſuch a pair of ſparkling eyes, as would
foil the diamond of its luſtre, and do more
execution than a thouſand officers of
juſtice at the *home ſtroke*; they are remarkably brilliant in their water, and
ſhed ſuch rays of delight as pierce the
ſoul of the dying gazer, and melt him,
down to the genial tranſport ; her breaſts
are well formed (though rather ſmall)
to contribute to the joy, and will ſwell
with emulation to rival the fulleſt pair in
the amorous conflict. She is actively
wanton

wanton in awaking or heightening every
pleasure her *temple* affords, and though
backward in *receiving* the *offerings*, yet
loves to receive the *good things secretly* and
in the *fullest* manner, for which her *sanc-
tum sanctorum* is admirably adapted.
Her temper is not to be found fault with,
so very good natured indeed, as never to
refuse a guinea oblation from any of her
sacrificers, that is, if she is convinced
they cannot afford her two.

Miss Br—wn, No. 2, *Little Chapel
Street.*

" Beware the magic of her eyes,
" For there the artful Cupid lies.

This young lady has not been above
two years a convert to her present profession, and is said to have received her
first instructions from a near relation,
who is since gone to Ireland, of which
country he is a native. She is about
eighteen, short and thick, has red hair
and light eyes, good teeth, fair skin,
pretty face and blooming cheeks. She
is very fond of singing, and has a good
voice, is very earnest in her pursuit
after

after the fport, and dreffes very gay.
One thing is greatly againft her, and
may poffibly reduce her fooner than fhe
may imagine, that is, fhe is too fond of
a glafs of ftrong water. Her expectations are very moderate.

Mifs B—rer—ft, No. 16, New
Compton Street.

Were I the lord o'er this terraqueous globe,
I'd give the whole for one luxurious night,—
Enfolded in thy arms ; nor envy Kings,
Their royal fairs ; for in thy looks,
Such heav'nly beauty, with fuch goodnefs dwells,
That every charm, an angel can command,
Summ'd up in thee—at once falute the heart.

A young founcellor is fuppofed to be
the keeper of this fmart little prattler,
though it is well known, that in her
court there are many befides the counfellor fuffered to plead ; her court might
be termed the court of *Common Pleafe*, although no Writs of Error are allowed ;
every member pays his fee in the fame
kind of coin, no coin but one being
current there. It is well known, this
lady

lady has two particular friends, befides
the counfellor ; and fo well does fhe con-
trive matters, that each in fucceffion enjoys the lovely fair, and thinks her all
his own; fhe fings a good fong, plays
the piano forte with grace and judgment,
and is an accomplifhed dancer : Is now
in her eighteenth year, not very fhort,
nor yet *very* fat, neither is fhe *very* pretty
but has a *very* fair complexion, *very* fine
eyes, and *very* fair hair, and is of a *very*
pleafing and *very* good temper. She is
alfo *very* new on the town, being only of
three months ftanding ; whoever wifhes
to fee this very defirable girl muft behave
themfelves in a *very* polite manner, after
which kind of treatment fhe has *very* little
objections to meet you at any proper
houfe of affignation, where, with a *gou*
peculiar to herfelf, fhe will give you fuch
a treat of voluptuous enjoyment, fuch a
feaft of amorous delight, that you fhall
fay with pleafure, in the words of a celebrated Poet.

Ungrateful Time to chafe away the night,
Did with his fcythe make pinions for his feet.

Mifs

Miss R—h M—rc—r, No. 9, *Holland Street.*

Ralpho was mounted now, and gotten,
O'erthwart his breast, with active vaulting;
Wriggling his body to recover,
His seat, and cast his right leg over.

This person generally goes by the name of my lady, not from any natural deformity of body, or any nobility of blood that runs in her veins, but a nickname which was given to her in her youthful days, from her extravagance of dress, which however at present is much reduced, indeed of late she has procured an addition to her title, which was that of " light finger," for the propriety of which we must refer to a certain Mercer in Cranbourn alley, whose cost and trouble in proving her ladyship's title, no doubt he will never forget. An excess of exercise in her line, has not a little impaired her person, tho' she has yet something agreeable about her, before she has consulted the bottle too much, for when inebriated, her temper is most turbulent; and she has passions which outstrip the wind. She is of the larger size both in regard to height and corpulence;

fence ; has black hair and eyes, fpeaks
gruff, is very amorous, and very moderate In her demands. Her age is about
twenty fix, and her favorite is as noted
as any *Horfeman* whatever.

Mifs Kitty P——t, No. 4, *Union Street,*
Middlefex Hofpital.

Within each others arms let's fink to reft ;
Thy eyes fhall make my days ferene and bright;
Thy arms, thus clinging round me, blefs the
    night.

As pride is reprefented to have been
the fall of many a one in former days,
fo in humble imitation of her ancef-
tors, it has not a little facilitated to
bring this lady to her prefent employment ; her parents ufed to drefs her up
in a higber ftile than her expectations
could by any means entitle her to,
which foon got the afcendency over her
morals, fo that as fhe grew up fhe determined rather than not to keep up her
ufual gaiety, fhe would fuffer proftitu-
tion. Within thefe few weeks, fhe has
been what perhaps has tended to facilitate her otherwife natural inclination.—
                              Viz.

Viz. a gallant lady's maid, as they are now termed by the fisterhood. She lodges very genteel, sees a deal of company, and dresses neat and decently ; her face is but homely, yet by the assistance of art she looks pretty well by candle light. She is thick and of low stature, good shape, easy carriage, and full of chat, tho' of but weak intellects ; her hair is light colour, as is also her eyes. She is about eighteen, *has* a good skin, and an even pretty set of teeth. Her price is as much as you please above one pound one.

Miss Y—ng, No. 5, *Chapel Street.*

" Coy and Covetous."

This lady's father was a native of Bologne in France, and came over to England some years ago, where he died ; she is however perfectly English in her language and manners ; and tho' rampant in her desires, puts on a particular coyness, in order to make her admirers the more eager. She is very covetous of money, and generally has

L   a good

a good price for her favours, one way or other, (a word to the wife.) She is in statue, short and thick, her face has something pretty in it, tho' her features are very small, her hair is a light brown, her eyes grey, her teeth indifferent, and breath offensive, but she has a good skin, and is not more than five and twenty.

Miss Cl—k, No. 34, Union Street.

Is a lady, who seems to possess a very great inclination for the mysteries of the Cyprian deity, she hath been for sometime a devout worshipper to the great grief of her mother, who took no small pains to instil into her the principles of religion and virtue; her father has been dead sometime, whose incontinency to the marriage bed may account in some measure for the vicious inclinations of the daughter, he having ruined his wife and constitution by his propensity to the sport of Venus; from which we use the old motto with some degree of justice, " What is bred in the bone will never " come out of the flesh." She is not handsome,

handfome, rather ordinary features, a
little pitted with the fmall pox, light
hair and grey eyes, and in fact has no
great recommendation, but her youth.

Mifs M—y Ann M—ck—y, at Mr.
R—s, a Shoemaker in *Oxford Street*.

Well pleas'd at the *frolic*, fhe laugh'd at the pain,
And wifh'd with more ardor to try it again;
Which when handled and dandled, and made fit
    for ufe,
She pufh'd with lefs pain as the parts were more
    loofe;
Then *upping* and *downing*, kind nature told how,
She cry'd, over-raptur'd, it does not hurt now.

This little flim lafs is daughter of a
late under gardener to the Duke of
N ———d, and was the darling of her
parents, who brought her up in the utmoft pride imaginable, although they
knew they had not a penny to give her,
as befides her they had feveral other
children. At about feventeen fhe eloped with the niece of a perfon in the
neighbourhood, and took lodgings near
Dean-ftreet, Soho, where they were
both traced by their relations, who took
L 2   them

them home again, and confined them
for some time, but no sooner had they
got their liberty but they eloped again,
and soon became professed courtezans.
The companion of Miss M———y
soon caught the small-pox and died,
but Miss Mary Ann pursued her way in
the path of Venus, being for a while as
gay a lady as any about the Town, but
is now reduced to traffic in a more re-
tired manner. She is rather short, and
a little out in one shoulder, has dark
hair and fine black eyes, a dark skin,
and somewhat pitted with the small
pox. Her age is about twenty six, and
she is not extravagant in her demands.

Mrs. D—x—n, No. 9, *Holland Street.*

Thus our chief joys with most alloys are curst,
And our best things, when once corrupted worst.

As this lady has received favours
from an officer in the navy, we shall
describe her in the marine stile. She
is an old ship in the service, and has
been cruising for several years, but is
very little damaged, and is reckoned a
prime

prime failor, notwithftanding fhe has had many a broadfide poured in upon her; and tho' fhe has been attack'd fore and aft, has always efcaped being totally fired ; altho' now and then a little burnt in the midfhips, fhe has been often boarded, and has but feldom fprung a leak : She is reckoned to carry a fine bowfprit, and is near fix feet from head to ftern. Some think fhe carries her main-top-fail too high, her rigging fome months ago was very much fhattered, but was refitted at the expence of Capt. ———, And notwithftanding fhe is in the Englifh fervice, fometimes wears foreign flags: being fond of putting in among the African ports, vulgarly call'd the black hops : She will fail with any one into the harbour of pleafure for the price of what fhe can bargain for.

———

Mifs N—wt—n, No. 22, *New Compton Street, St. Giles's.*

The diftinction of this lady's fex is faid to be fomewhat equivocal; but, as to our knowledge, fhe carries on a bufy trade. We fhall content ourfelves

in

in confidering her a woman *only*, as then
we piefume and hope we fhall be right.
Her dependence is almoft entirely on *elderly vifitors*, who are at *moft* times *moft*
acceptable to the fifterhood, for her appearance would procure her very little
cuftom, from what the ladies call the
pad, as fhe might very reafonably be taken for what is called an old maid, for
from the general ftile of her drefs, fhe
only ftands in need of a ruff, to realize
the reprefentation of the print of Peter
Paul Rubens's wife; yet her drefs is always neat, and fhe keeps her fkin remarkable clean; her features are homely, and
fhe has a very dead eye; but from her
extenfive knowledge and practice in the
Metaphyfical Doctrine of *Venus's Tactics*,
fhe reduces every thing to *logical certainty*,
and preferves an excellent name among
thofe gentry whom the celebrated mother Mitchel calls *rum codger's*. She is
about twenty four, fhort in ftature, and
a fair complexion.

Mifs Mo---re, at Mrs. W—ds—rs.
King's Place.

Whate'er the man of pleafure would command
Wherein a miftrefs blefs'd with every charm

May shew her fondness, and make known her love,
And then with kind embracements, tempting
  kisses,
Sink her declining head into his bosom,
And ask with silent words—*a woman's gift*,
Which, being close conveyed beneath her shift
And harbour'd in the *port* of full delight,
She'll pour profusely all her *liquid store*.

Those who have luscious palates, will
not here be disappointed, for this is a
very vivacious agreeable girl, with all the
vivid fire of untamed youth shooting
through her veins, and electrifying not
only her whole frame, but the coldest and
most non-electric body that can come in
contact with her; the shock however,
is so poignantly rapturous, that he who
has once bathed in her *Elysian fountain*,
would wish to repeat the luxuriant *lave*,
and gratify every sense with unutterable
bliss. Her eyes are of a beautiful sparkling blue, and beam a torrent of light at
every potent glance. She has good teeth;
her breasts are in the fullest proportion,
and will rebound with the most grateful
ardor to the hand's soft pressure. For
such a girl, sure a couple of guineas is the
merest trifle to a man of pleasure.
          Mrs.

Mrs. H---pk---ns, No 11, *Little Castle Yard, Holborn.*

Not Cæsar's emprefs would fhe deign to prove;
No : make her miftrefs to the man fhe loves,
·Love, free as air, at fight of human ties,
Spreads his light wings, and in a moment flies;
Let wealth, let honour wait the wedded dame,
Auguft her deed, and facred be her fame:
Before ftrong paffion all thofe views remove,
Fame, Wealth, and Honour, what are ye to Love?

An agreeable nymph in all the bloom
of womanhood, cannot fail of pleafing
the moft difficult, and of warming even
conftitutional coldnefs into genial pleafure. Such then is Mrs H---, and fuch fhe
is, that every young defire might here be
nurfed to tranfport, for never was a richer
bed for them to revel in, than the fwelling foftnefs of her downy body; her
breafts filled with the milky tubes of nature, and warm with the vital current of
each purple vein, rife into two fuch femi-
globes that the happy poffeffor of their
world of fweets, need not envy a Cæ-
far the more capacious earthly globe;
for how fuperior is love to ambition, and
the poffeffion of a lovely object for one
night, *ftands* higher in the *eye* of pleafure,
                                        than

than to wield the fceptre of the greateft
monarchy for a year.---What can equal
the *tumid fceptre* of amorous delight? nothing in this charmer's *eye*, the rofy tints
of whofe cheeks, and the pouting ruby
of her delicately parted lips mock the
whole affemblage of the gay creation, and
defy the faireft of the fair to vie with
them. She has expreffive dark eyes,
brown hair, and teeth not altogether
unpleafing. She is fhort and plump,
mild temper, and of a moft generous difpofition; fo that the true votary of the
Cyprian God, and full of the *liquid balm,*
need not be deterred from vifiting her,
from any pecuniary fear. It is faid a certain North Briton, who is connected with
a capital iron manufactory, is her chief
fupporter, he having taken, and furnifhed
for her the houfe fhe now occupies.

Mifs W---nt---r, at Mrs. Kelly's, *Duke
ftreet, St. James's.*

Our *fouls* their former joys renew,
   We raife new fport and wanton gefting,
Our eyes each others charms review,
   In every form of love contefting;

At

At laft, our bodies warm'd with mutual fire,
    To prove each others aid, to *join in one*
    conſpire.

'Tis not an eaſy matter to come at the
real names of many of thoſe ladies, who
have enliſted under the Banners of Venus,
ſome taking upon them fictitious ones
thro' fear, others thro' modeſty, in regard
to their family, and others thro' oſten-
tation to pretend to have connection with
ſome great folks, to whom they have not
the moſt diſtant affinity. We have been
credibly informed, that the preſent character aſſumes a name which is not real,
but has done it on account of her own
being of High Germanic origin of which
Country ſhe is a native. She is rather
tall and luſty, but very genteel, has a
regular ſet of features, blooming cheek,
fine light hair and eyes, is very chatty,
and pleaſing in her behaviour. Her age
doth not exceed five and twenty, and
her expectations are not unreaſonable.

Miſs L—ttr—ll, No 13, *Wardour Street.*

Thy fatal eyes my beſt reſolves betray,
My anger melts in ſoft deſires away ;

Each

Each look, each glance, for all thy crimes attone,
Eludes my rage, and I'm again undone.

She was the daughter of a fan maker
in Dublin, and was dreſſed up by her
ſtep-mother, who was very fond of her,
in hopes of drawing ſome young man of
fortune in for her huſband: but alaſs!
poor Betſey was taken in herſelf, by a
young fellow of the college, who took
her away, kept her in his chambers for
two days, and then turned her off, with
remembrance, that gave her great pain, and
has left the marks of the ſurgeon's ſciſſars
by which ſhe may be known on a cloſe
inſpection. The cutting reproaches of
her parents, for a fault which their own
vanity had cauſed, rendered Ireland
irkſome to her, and ſhe gladly accompanied her father to England, where he
came on buſineſs, and promiſed to ſet-
tle her with ſome relations, till the noiſe
of her firſt ſlip had blown over in Dublin. But he, unfeeling man! left her in
the country to ſubſiſt as ſhe could. Thus
turned adrift to the wide world, ſhe
came to Liverpool, and being young
and handſome, got good buſineſs
amongſt the young tradeſmen and ſea
captains, till ſhe took to drinking to
drown

drown thought. At length her face having become familiar to every eye, she came up to London, where she has been about three years. She is really a fine figure, and about twenty five; with dark hair and eyes, her complexion is not of the fairest, but she has tolerable teeth, and may be had at an easy expence.

Miss Nancy W—lm—t, No. 38, *Union Street, Middlesex Hospital.*

Reclin'd upon a couch the maiden lay,
And all her Virgin Charms expos'd to view;
I saw them all, unseen, and in her eyes
Read the mad language of untaught desire.

Never sure was any one more fond of the tremulating business of love, than is this lively lass; she was sent for out of Warwickshire to attend an old aunt, who intended to leave her very handsomely when she died, but being deluded by the arts of a young fellow in the neighbourhood, which was discovered by the prominence of her belly, her aunt turned her out of doors. After her delivery, the child dying, and
her

her feducer turning her off, fhe was
obliged by neceffity to do the beft fhe
could for herfelf. She is about twenty,
very fair, good teeth, middling fized,
and genteel to follow, but not fo agreeable to meet. She keeps the houfe, and
alfo (what is but too common among the
fifterhood) her flafh man, who chief-
ly refides with her.

Mifs W—ll—s, No. 11, *Little Caftle
Yard, Holborn.*

> Her lips to mine how often hath fhe join'd,
> Between each kifs her oaths of true-love fwearing,
>   How many tales to pleafe me hath fhe coin'd,
> Dreading my love the lofs thereof ftill fearing,
>   Yet in the midft of all her pure proteftings,
> Her faith, her oaths, her tears, and all were
>   jeftings:

It is pity that the moft charming part
of the creation, the delight of mankind,
and the fweetners of human life, whofe
beauty enlivens and calls forth every
fenfation of the foul, exhilirates the fpirits, wakes every latent fpring into action, throws a luftre upon, and enlight-
M   ens

ens thofe fcenes which would otherwife
be morofe and gloomy, and fheds a foft
emanation on the mind of man, fweetly
harmonizing it to downy pleafure, and
moulding the warm heart to every genial joy. It is pity that fuch powerful,
pleafing, and endearing qualities, fhould
have for their alloy fuch an unpleafing,
difgufting, and ungrateful one, as in-
conft▓▓▓ and capricioufnefs, too generally the concomittant attendant on
the fex. Such a one, unfortunately for
herfelf, is the fair in queftion, who was
reduced from a ftate of grandeur to her
prefent fituation, by the natural inconftancy of her difpofition; too openly
abufing the kindeft keepers, and thofe
who would have maintained her in a
ftate of fplendor, being now glad of any
body's favours. Though fhe is tall and
very well made, of tolerable beauty,
a fair complexion, and a pair of eyes
which outfparkle the diamonds of Gol-
condo, and is of a good difpofition, very
chatty and converfible. Her age is
about two and twenty,

(123)

Miſs H—d—e, at Mrs. R——s, No. 7, Wardour Street.

But ſtill the lovely maid improves her charms,
Wi;h inward greatneſs, unaffected wiſdom,
And ſanctity of manner.

Although this lady cannot be ſtiled a
perfect beauty, ſtill I think ſhe well
deſerves theſe lines of Mr. Addiſon's.
Her genuine wit and vivacity, her
lively diſpoſition, and pretty flow of
words, which never poſſeſs the leaſt
tinge of vulgarity, having been brought
up by Lady B—— of Argile Street,
her truly amiable temper and ſurpaſſing
good-nature, plead in conjunction ſo
very powerfully, and add ſo many
charms to every feature, that you can
no longer look without loving. She is
now in her nineteenth year, with well-
formed firm breaſts, fair complexion, a
natural good bloom, a ſet of ſmall, re-
gularly placed, white teeth, a little of
the crumby caſt, which does not extend
beyond a *deſirable* plumpneſs or deprive
her in *bed* from making a *deſirable fellow*,
at which time ſhe never wants mutual
feeling. Her tongue and eyes have then
declined corporeal language, and ſeem
only to dictate a rapturous cement of

M 2   ſouls.

fouls. She will repeat the pleafure as often as you *pleafe*, but ftill is often known to give *out* firft. Her eyes are light, altho' her hair is of a fine dark auburn, and fhe is feldom prefented with lefs than two pounds two, having been but very lately initiated into the order of the fifterhood.

Mifs T—lb—t, at Mrs. Sp———r, *Bury Street, St James's.*

Warm fancy flutters with her airy wing,

And in my bofom points her madd'ning fling;

Nerves my ftrong purpofe, to unnerve the ftrength,

Of many a man and lay him at full length.

This victorious Amazon, whofe prow-efs has many a time been tried in the *amorous field*, is exceedingly well calcu-lated, from the ftrength of her *parts*, and ardor of her inclination, to humble the *pride* of man, and when fhe has him once on his knees, fhe never fails to make him *yield* himfelf thoroughly van-quifhed, though at the fame time (whe-ther out of infult or no we leave to be de-termin ed

termined by thofe who have *engaged* her;
fhe will ufe her every endeavour to *raife*
her fallen *antagonift* up again, and leave
no manual inducement unpracticed to
make him *ftand up ftiff* againft her, it is
very lately fhe came from Ireland,
where fhe was in good keeping by a
military officer. She is a fine girl, tall
and well limb'd, has a pretty face, dark
eyes and hair, good teeth, and about
five and twenty. We are told fhe thinks
herfelf well worth five guineas for a
thorough engagement in the war's of
Venus.

Mifs Br—ce Mack—z—e, No. 44
Gloucefter Court, St. James's Street.

When my folds of blifs unfold,
Joys too mighty to be told,
Tafte what extafies they give,
Dying raptures tafte, and live;
In my ——, difdaining meafure;
Come and pour in all thy treafure;
Soft defires that fweetly languifh,
Fierce delights that rife to anguifh.

M 3   This

This lovely brunette has what we may call rather a handfome than a pretty perfon, and a pair of fpeaking dark eyes which throws a certain becomingnefs over a remarkable frefh rofy complexion ; for the expreffion which they convey is fired with all the wantonnefs of untamed defire, and wakes the coldeft fenfe to the rapturous delights of Venus, who never had a warmer votary than this voluptuous daughter of pleafure. Her bofom is full zoned, and each living font, fupplied from a thoufand lactiferous tubes, rifes inftantaneous to the flighteft touch, and recedes and heaves alternately with the involuntary *feelings* of the titillating power ; infomuch that fhe is entitled, and well known by the name of '' hard bubbies.'' Her hair is of a dark brown, and thick enough to form feveral beautiful treffes, which however are not equal to the *tufted grove* on the *mount below* ; and the well-fhaded borders of the *bower of blifs*, reared upon two living columns of alabafter, that would fhame the whiteft Parifian marble; then how lovely the contraft! between thefe fnow-white pillars, the dark umbrageous appearance invefting the *magic circle*, and the ruby tinge on the infide

of

of each *portal lip,* which pouting out
with incontroulable fenfibility, enclofes
the *member* of all its joys, in fo right a
direction, there never needs any pilot
to conduct the pinnace to the very *port*
of blifs. Notwithftanding this, fhe is
fo exceedingly frifky, from being fo exquifitely toned in thofe parts, that you
will furely be thrown out of the *faddle,*
though ever fo good a *rider,* and the
courfe half won ; for enjoyment rifes fo
near to madnefs with her, and the *rapturous anguifh* is fo great, that fhe will
endeavour, though againft her will, to
wriggle you out of her *hole* with her bottom, and at the fame time give you the
moft delicious fqueezes with her thighs,
accompanied with an enchanting twift
of her legs, to drive you *further in;* and
when the *critical moment is coming,* fhe
contrives to meet the *fucculent fhower*
half way, by *pouring* down a copious
ftream of the fame *life-giving fluid* from
every *fpring within her,* till both lie
bathed in *liquid* blifs—

In extafies too great to laft for ever.

This maddening fportive fair one has a
fet of teeth like ivory, is very good natured

tured, and not in keeping, but lives on
the bounty of her various good friends
in that vicinity, among whom it is
whifpered there has been a certain royal
H—— apparent and the gallant Colonel
T———.

She is tall and plump, and her age
doth very little exceed twenty years.

Mifs L—ngf—d, No. 10, *Cumberland
Street, Middlefex Hofpital.*

" Softnefs of fpeech, and opennefs of heart,
" Combine with love to act the am'rous part."

A young lady very genteel, finely
limbed, and though fhe has rather an
aufterity of countenance, fhe confers
delight like the fun behind a cloud,
imperceptibly clears up, and fhines
with a brightnefs fcarce to be conceived
which, added to a moft cheerful manner
of converfation, and a natural turn for
repartee, makes her one of the moft
agreeable ladies that ever enlifted under
the banners of the Cyprian goddefs.
Yorkfhire has the honour of claiming
her birth, and I am forry to fay a certain

tain new-created Peer had the dishon-
our of debauching one who by nature
was formed to be the ornament of her
fex, the repeated brutal villainy which
brought this unhappy girl to her prefent
way of life would make the moft har-
dened blufh, therefore I muft drop my
pen after defcribing more particularly
her perfon. She is tall and genteel,
has fine flaxen hair, blue fparkling eyes,
and arch'd eye-brows, the foft blufh of
Aurora over-fpreads her cheeks, and
the Lilly may be obferved difplayed on
her enchanting bofom, which is finely
inlaid with blue veins. She has till very
lately been in keeping by a gentleman
of her prefent name, who has paid the
laft debt of nature. She is about two
and twenty, and her expectations are no
ways extravagant.

Mifs G—dfr—y, No. 23, *Union Street.*

" Form'd to the fport, fhe knows her cue,
" And will in love return each one his due."

A fonder little tit is not to be met
with in all the kingdom; in the ac-
tio n

tion she will twist about like an eel, and will practife every ftratagem that is to be found in the records of love, to give and receive pleafure : fhe has a remarkable foft hand, the warmth of which has often been tried ; and, as if it was endowed with miraculous powers, it has been known to raife the dead ! She is faid to be a daughter of a gentlewoman who keeps a fchool in the fame neighbourhood, and was very lately introduced to the fervice of the public, to whom fhe is now fervently devoted, and by whofe generofity fhe is enabled to live in a very gay manner, having fel- dom a lefs compliment than two guineas. She is of a flim and genteel fize, well fhaped, has fair hair and light eyes, good teeth, and is very fprightly. Her age is about nineteen.

Mifs

Mifs H—ll, at No. 4, *Caſtle Street*, *Oxford Market*.

O that I had but Jove's unbounded might,
To lengthen pleaſures, and extend the night,
Three trivial nights ſhould not my wiſh con-
    fine ;
Whole years themſelves, whole ages ſhould
    combine
To make my joys as laſting as divine.
Then would I lie enclos'd within her arms,
Fierce as my love, and vig'rous as her charms,
And both ſhould be, could I decree their ſtate,
As fixed and as immutable as fate.

Of all the ſiſterhood we know, Miſs
H—ll is the moſt modeſt, delicate, and
mild, and has leaſt the appearance of
one of Venus's exprefs votaries. Her perſon is tall, ſlim and genteel, her face is
agreeable, though not handſome. Her
voice is charming, and her eyes lively,
She is about twenty one, of good temper and winning behaviour. She hath
had ſome few particular friends, none
of whom, ſhe ever loſt through her own
miſconduct, but from the natural incon-
ſtancy of mankind, being but very
lately entered into life. A foreign gentleman has her now in keeping, who
from

from being fond of her is rather jealous.
However three guineas is a temptation
not to be withftood by many better fitu-
ated than herfelf.

Mifs Ell—t, No. 16, *Glanville Street.*

You may admire the rofes on my cheek,
And prefs my lips, which balmy nectar fpeak!
Admire my eyes, that beam with liquid fire;
My breafts which part with foft yet ftrong de-
     fire;
Admire my legs; admire my fnowy thighs;
But know, my pleafure in the center lies;
There prefs with willing force the tumid gueft,
And let luxurious fancy paint the reft.

An apt motto for this truly amorous
girl, who confines her whole pleafure to
the *central fpot* of Nature. Here, if
poffible, fhe will keep you conftantly
employed, nor fpare any pains by *manual, lingual, labial* invitations, to revivify the fallen member, and with glowing eagernefs, will quickly bring him
to *Death's door*, where that is foon his
portion. She is a well-made tall,
                brown

brown girl, has very good teeth, dark
hair and eyes, not more than five and
twenty years of age, and in her manner
remarkably lively and genteel. She
is well worth a guinea per diem.

AGREE-

AGREEABLE to annual cuſtom, we muſt now bid adieu to our courteous reader, and wiſh him every ſucceſs that youth, health, love, and wine can poſſibly inſpire him with; hoping at the ſame time, that they will throw a friendly veil over all the unavoidable errors that may have happened in this work, and excuſe that diſagreeable tautology, which, for want of other words, we are neceſſitated to make, and ſhould they find the ſame ladies in this liſt, that appeared before in other names, not be diſpleaſed with it; for as their reſidence is changed as often as their names, it is almoſt impoſſible but ſome ſuch miſtakes muſt happen : We alſo hope that the attention that is now paid to the procuring the beſt and moſt reſpectable, will wipe off every other blot.

We likewiſe take our leave of the Ladies, and are particularly happy to think that what was formerly ſeen in the eyes of *our* world a diſgrace, is now conſidered, pleaſing, delightful, and honourable.

F I N I S.

In questo libro dove a[.....]
le [....]e le più celebri o rogate
[...]i di Londra, e descritte
particolarmente [....] [.....],
to che [.......]

HARRIS's LIST

O F

Covent Garden Ladies,

For the YEAR 1788.

[Price 2s. 6d.]

Harris

HARRIS's LIST

O F

COVENT-GARDEN LADIES:

● R,

MAN OF PLEASURE's

K A L E N D E R,

For the YEAR, 1788.

CONTAINING

The Histories and some curious Anecdotes of the most celebrated Ladies
now on the Town, or in keeping, and
also many of their Keepers.

———————

L O N D O N:

Printed for H. RANGER, (formerly at No. 23,
Fleet-Street,) at No. 9, *Little Bridges-Street,* near
Drury-Lane Play-House

Where may be had,

The seperate L i s t s of many preceding Years

CONTENTS.

A.

G

(x)

ERRATA.

In page 42, Mifs Cl—nt—n, at No.
17, *read* ——— Street.
Page 72 *read* No. 4, *inftead* of No.
14.
Page 77, *read* Mrs L—w—s, at No. 68,

ERRATA,

INTRODUCTION.

Again the coral berry'd holly glads the eye,
The ivy green again each window decks,
And misletoe, kind friend to *Baffia's* caufe,
Under each merry roof invites the kifs;
Come then, my friends, ye friends to *Harris* come,
And more than kiffes fhare, drink love fupreme
From his ambrofial cup, tho' oft replete
Satiety ne'er gives, but leaves the ravifh'd fenfe
Supremely bleft, and ever craving more.
Come ye gay fons of pleafure, come and feaft
Your *every* fenfe, and lave your fouls in love,
Fearlefs advance, nor think of ills to come;
Here tafte variety, of love's fweet gifts,
Pure and unftain'd as at kind nature's birth.

THE parterre of Venus was never
more elegantly filled, never did
the loves and graces fhine with more
fplendor than at prefent; Mary bone,
the now grand paradife of love, and
Covent Garden, her elder born, beam
with uncommon ardor; nor is our
antient Drury unfrequented; no fooner
do the ftars above fhed their benign influence, but our more attracting ones
B   below

below befpangle every walk, and make
a heaven on earth; Bagnigge, St. George's
Spa, with all their fifter fhops, deal
out each night their choiceft gifts of love;
nor with the fons of pleafure be difappointed fhould they extend their travels
ftill farther eaft, and vifit the purlieus
of White Chapel: The Royalty is
over full, and Wapping, Shadwell, and
the neighbouring *fields* lend all their
lovely train to glad each night; thefe
then fhall be our walks; from thefe gay
fpots of pleafure fhall we call love's
pureft fweets,

And without thorn the rofe.

By thus extending our refearches we
fhall be able to fuit every conftitution,
and every pocket, every whim and
fancy that the moft extravagant fenfualift can defire. Here may they learn to
fhun the dreadful quickfands of pain and
mortification, and land fafe on the terra
firma of delight and love.

HARRIS's LIST

OF

COVENT-GARDEN LADIES.

Mifs L—ft---r, No. 6, *Union-Street,*
Oxford-Road.

Oh, pleafing tafk, to paint the ripen'd charms
Of youth untutor'd in the female arts ;
To fee inftinctively defire blaze out,
And warm the mind with all its burning joys.
The *tell-tale eyes* in liquid pools fuftain'd,
The throbbing breaft now rifing, now fuppreff'd ;
The *thrilling blifs* quick darting thro' the frame,
The *fhort fetch'd fighs,* the fnow white twining
  limbs,
The fudden gufh, and the extatic oh.

SUCH our all pleafing L—-ft—-r
leads the train, and, fmiling like
the morn, unfolds her heaven of beauties.
Oh, for a *Guido's touch,* or *Thomfon's*
B 2   *thought,*

thought, to paint the richnefs of her
unequall'd charms; every perfection
that can poffibly adorn the face and
mind of woman feem centered in this bewitching girl ; hither refort then, ye
genuine lovers of beauty and good
fenfe ; here, whilft *Plutus* reigns, may
you revel nor know fatiety ; here feaft
the longing appetite, and return with
frefh *vigor* to every *attack*. Now arrived
at the tempting age of nineteen, her imagination is filled with every lufcious
idea, *refined* fenfibility, and *fierce defire*
can unite, her form is majeftic, tall, and
elegant ; her make truly genteel, her
complexion

———— As April's lily fair,
And blooming as June's brighteft rofe.

Painted by the mafterly hand of nature,
fhaded by treffes of the darkeft brown,
and enlivened by two ftars that fwim in
all the effence of unfatiated love.

Her pouting lips diftil nectarious balm,
And thro' the frame its thrilling tranfports
dart ;

which, when parted, difplay a cafket
of fnow white pearls, ranged in the niceft
regularity, the *neighbouring hills* below
full

full ripe for manual preſſure, firm ; and elaſtic, and heave at every touch. The *Elyſian font*, in the centre of a *black bewitching grove*, ſupported by two pyramids white as alabaſter, very delicate, and ſoft as turtle's-down. At the *approach* of their *favourite lord* unfold, and for three guineas he is conducted to this *harbour* of never failing delight. Add to all this, ſhe ſings well, is a very chearful companion, and has only been in *life* nine months.

Miſs H—ll—nd, No. 2, *York-Street,*
Queen-Ann-ſtreet.

No time ſhall paſs without that dear delight,
I'll ta'k of love all day, and act it a'l the night;
Pleaſure and I as to one goal deſign'd,
Will run with equal pace, while ſorrow lays
    behind.

Thoſe who chooſe to ſail to the iſland of love in a *firſt rate* ſhip, or to encloſe an armful of delight, muſt be pleaſed with this lady ; who, tho' only ſeventeen and ſhort, is very fat and corpulent ; yet, notwithſtanding, ſhe is a fine piece of frailty ; her face is handſome, and

B 3   her

her *nut brown locks*, which are placed *above* and below, promise a luscious treat to the voluptuary. Her temper is agreeable and pleasing, and she is so far from being mercenary, that a single guinea is the boundage of her wish.

Miss B—rn, No. 18, *Old Compton Street, Soho.*

Close in the arms she languishingly lies,
With dying looks, short breath, and wishing
eyes.

This accomplished nymph has just attained her eighteenth year, and fraught with every perfection, enters a volunteer in the field of Venus. She plays on the piano forte, sings, dances, and is mistress of every *Manœuvre* in the amorous contest that can enhance the coming pleasure; is of the middle stature, fine auburn hair, dark eyes, and very inviting countenance, which ever seems to beam delight and love. In bed she is all the heart can wish, or eye admire, every limb is symmetry, every action under cover truly amorous; her price is two pounds two.

Mis

(19)

Miss J—nſ—n, No 17, *Goodge ſtreet,* *Charlotte ſtreet.*

And all theſe joys inſatiably to prove,
With which rich beauty feaſts the glutton love.

The raven coloured treſſes of Miſs
J—nſ—n are pleaſing, and are charac-
teriſtics of ſtrength and ability in the
wars of Venus. Indeed this fair one is
not afraid of work, but will undergo a
great deal of labour in the action; ſhe
ſings, dances, will drink a chearful glaſs,
and is a good companion. She has ſuch
a noble elaſticity in her loins, that ſhe can
caſt her lover to a pleaſing height, and
receive him again with the utmoſt dexterity. Her price is one pound one, and
for her perſon and amorous qualifications
ſhe is well worth the money.

Miſs L—v—r, No. 17, *Ogle ſtreet,* *Queen Ann-ſtreet Eaſt.*

She darted from her eyes a ſide long glance
Juſt as ſhe ſpoke, and, like her words, it flew,
Seem'd not to beg, what yet ſhe bid to do.

This young nymph of fifteen is
ſhort, of a dark complexion, and inclinable

able to be lufty; fhe does not rely on *chamber practice* only, for fhe takes her evening excurfions to feek for *clients*, who may put their cafe to her either in a tavern or her own apartments; her fee is from a crown to half a guinea, and fhe ftrives to earn her money by feeming to be agreeable; however, fhe may pleafe fome, and as we have only known her about four months fhe cannot have loft her *appetite*, but feems particularly fond of the fport.

Mifs L—nf—y, No. 13, *Bentick ftreet, Berwick ftrret.*

Clofe in the arms fhe languifhingly lies,
With dying looks, fhort breath, and fwimming eyes.

To all lovers of carrots we would recommend this fair complex, and blue ey'd nymph; fhe is now fteering into the nineteenth year, and has very little of the vulgarity too often found in the fifterhood, but would be rather filent than fpeak nonfenfe: the mere fenfualift will not find her quite to his fancy, but fhe will pleafe the delicate and fenfible, who can fpend the dull paufe of joy with her agreeably, till call'd by nature to repeti- tion, in which, as well as in confervation, we are informed fhe is equally charming.

Mifs H—rd—y, No. 45, *Newman fireet.*

Her look ferene does pureft fofness wear,
Her face exclaims her faireft of the fair.

This lady borrows her name from her late keeper, who is now gone to the In- dia's, and left her to feek fupport on the wide common of independance; fhe is now juft arrived at the zenith of perfec- tion, devoid of art and manners, as yet untutor'd by fafhion, her charms have for heir zeft every addition youth and fim- plicity can add. She has beauty with- out pride, elegance without affectation, and innocence without diffimulation; and not knowing how long this train of perfections will laft, we would advife our reader to make hay whilft the fun fhines.

Mifs

Miss Br—wn, No. 8, *Caftle-Street,*
Newman-Street.

Her every glance, like Jove's vindictive flame,
Shoot thro' the veins, and kindle all the frame,

A peculiar elegance in make and tafte
in drefling diftinguifhes this daughter of
love ; her fhape is remarkably genteel,
and her figure good ; fhe fings a good
fong, and is a chearful *bon* companion ;
her complexion is fair, her eyes, though
grey, exceedingly melting, and feem to
fpeak the difpofition of the parts below
very forcibly, and if you would wifh to
find a good bed-fellow, tho' not bleft
with every other perfection, this lady
will perhaps fuit her price, which is two
pounds two.

———————

Mrs. T—rb—t, No. 25, *Titchfield-ftreet.*

The glow of youth, the fire of wanton love,
Sport in her eye, and roufe the fenfual heart
To ftrong defires unmanageable pitch.

So univerfally known, and fo great a
fav'rite with the bucks is this lady, that
her defcription is almoft needlefs ; her
eyes and hair are of the moft inviting
darknefs,

darkneſs, her temper and diſpoſition
good, and her mind replete with the
choiceſt gifts of *Minerva*; her figure is
elegant, ſhe is very tall, ſings and dances
to perfection, and has only been in a
publit way of life twelve months; for a
ſingle ſkirmiſh ſhe does not refuſe the
King's ſmalleſt picture, but for a whole
night's ſiege expects three of the largeſt.

Miſs R—ch—rdſ—n, No. 2, *Bennett-
Street, Rathbone-Place.*

If women were as little as they are good,
A peas cod would make them a gown and a
    hood.

A pretty, little, lively, fair complexioned girl, with a dainty leg and foot,
and as pretty a pair of pouting bubbies
as ever went againſt a man's ſtomach,
and one who well deſerves the attention
that is paid her by every man capable of
knowing her value. She is pleaſing,
though fond, and can make wantonneſs
delightful; every part aſſiſts to bring on
the momentary delirium, and then each
part combines to raiſe up the fallen member, to contribute again to repeated
rapture; her price is commonly two gui-
                                        neas,

neas, but if the man is clever, she is very
ready to make some abatement.

Miss L—c—s, No. 2, *York-Street,*
Queen-Ann-Street East.

———— Liking o'er the lea,
Ye're welcomer to take me, than to let me be.

She is tall and fair, of a striking figure,
and amiable in conversation, perfectly
complying with the desires of her ena-
morato's: she is said, like the river
Nile, frequently to overflow, but some-
how or another her inundations differ
from those of that river, as they do not
produce fœcundity, some skilful gar-
deners are of opinion that she drowns
the *seed*, which is the reason that it does
not take root. This is a disagreeable
circumstance to those who may wish not
to till in vain ; but to others who would
prefer the pleasure without the expensive
consequences, she is the more desirable,
as they are sure that all who bathe in her
Castalian spring, will be overwhelmed
with a flood of delight.

Mrs.

Mrs. Cr—fby, No. 24, *George Street,*
over Black Fryars Bridge.

> Faſt lock'd in her armſ,
> And enjoying her charms,
> Every frown of old care I'll defy ;
> Give deſire ſuch a loofe,
> That the all potent *Juice,*
> Shall pervade ev'ry ſenſe, and *ſwim* in each
> Eye.

Birmingham lays claim to the birth of
this daughter of love, and, under the
care and protection of an indulgent
father and mother, ſhe reached her
fifteenth year " pure and unſullied ;"
at this period nature began to be very
buſy with Nancy, and a ſtrong propen-
ſity for ſeeing *Life,* compelled her to
leave her parents and enter into ſervitude,
and being particularly attached to the
ſons of Neptune, ſhe choſe for her
maſter a ſea captain, whoſe name ſhe
ſtill prefers to any other.   A twelve
month had not elapſed in the captain's
ſervice before our charmer's feelings had
reached their higheſt pitch, and the
captain, bleſt with a keen appetite, after
a ſix months voyage, with little perſua-
ſion, opened her *port hole,* cleared her
gangway, and threw her virtue *overboard.*

C   He

He grew ſtrongly attached to her, and,
being a man rather advanced in years,
became contented and happy, nor
wiſhed for any other but his dear Nancy.
She was his own, and he was all ſhe at
that time wiſhed or deſired for ; one or
two little prattlers were pledges of their
mutual regard, and till the day of the
captain's death they lived " the happy
pair." It is near two years ſince ſhe
loſt her friend, by whoſe death ſhe
receives a little annuity, that will ever
keep her from the neceſſity of parading
the ſtreets *merely* for ſupport, and you
are certain to meet with her at home at
almoſt any hour of the day ; in the
evening ſhe generally viſits one of the
Theatres, and always ſits in the ſide
boxes, in which place ſhe contrives to
chuſe her ſpark, and if poſſible to take
him home with her (for ſhe nevers ſleeps
out,) where he will meet with ſnug comfortable apartments, civility, good humour, and a very engaging partner,
whilſt ſhe continues good humoured ; if
he uſes any language or behaviour to
ruffle her temper, ſhe can act the Virago
as well as moſt of her ſex. She is rather
below mediocrity in ſize, with dark hair,
flowing in ringlets down her back,

languiſhing

languifhing grey eyes, and a very tolerable complexion, and a pair of pretty
little firm *bubbies*. Her leg and foot is
particularly graceful, always ornamented
with a white filk ftocking, and a neat
fhce ; fhe is a loving bed-fellow, and
fincerely *attaches* herfelf to the enjoyment,
feels the fhrilling fenfation with poignancy, and for one guinea will *enjoy* you
as many times as you pleafe.

N. B. She keeps the houfe, and you
muft not mention to her a fyllable con-
cerning her pretty lodger *above*, if you
wifh to be calm *below*.

Mifs Harriet J—n—-s, *St. George's
Hotel, oppofite Virginia Street, Wapping.*

For lips to lips, and Tongue to Tongue,
Will make a man of fixty young.

Yes, 'tis Harriet, the ftill fair, ftill
blooming Harriet, whofe eyes are
molded for the tender union of fouls (let
them but borrow a little fire from
Bacchus) "by Heaven's, fhoot Suns"
whofe nectar-diftilling lips pour fweeteft
balm ; whilft the foft filent lingual intercourfe fhoots powerfully through all the
C 2   frame,

frame, and awakes each dormant fenfe.
When naked fhe is certainly Thomfon's
Lavinia.

For lovelinefs,

Needs not the foreign aid of ornament,

But is, when unadorned, adorned the moft.

A beautiful *black fringe* borders the
Venetian Mount, and whether fhe purfues
the *Grabamatic* method from a practical
knowledge of its increafe of pleafure,
from motives of cleanlinefs, or as a certain preventative we will not pretend to
fay ; but we well know it makes her the
more defirable bed-fellow, and after
every *ftroke* gives frefh *tone and vigour* to
the lately *diftended parts* ; her legs and
feet claim her peculiar attention, nor do
their *coverings* ever difgrace their owner,
nor their actions under *cover* ever do
injuftice to that dear delightful fpot they
are doomed to fupport, protect, and pay
juft obedience to ; *the eager twine*, the
almoft unbearable prefs at the *dye away
moment*, with all *love's* leffer *Artillery*, fhe
plays off with uncommon activity and
ardor, and drinks *repetition* with thirft
infatiable. Half a guinea, and a new
pink ribband to encircle her bewitching
brows, is the leaft fhe expects for a night's
entertainment.

entertainment. There are three or four
more ladies of *our* order in the houfe, if
this lady fhould not exactly fuit.

But being bleft with beauty's potent fpell,
Muft from her other fifters bear the bell.

Mifs W—lk—nf—n, No. 10, *Bull-and-
Mouth Street.*

Forbidding me to follow fhe invites me,
This is the mould of which I made the fex,
I gave them but one tongue to fay us nay,
And two kind eyes to grant;

Here we prefent our readers with as
pretty a man's woman as ever the
bountiful hand of nature formed ; a
pair of black eyes that dart refiftlefs fire,
that fpeak a language frozen hearts
might thaw, and ftand as the fweet index
to the foul ; a pair of fweet pouting
lips that demand the burning kifs, and
never receives it without paying with
intereft ; a complexion that would charm
the eye of an anchorite ; a fkin fmooth
as monument alabafter, and white as
Alpian fnow ; and hair that fo beautifully contrafts the fkin, that nought
but nature can equal. Defcend a little
lower and behold the femi-fnow-balls.

C 3 " Studded

" Studded with rofe buds, and ftreaked
with celeftial blue,"

that want not the fupport of ftays;
whofe truly elaftic ftate never fuffers the
preffure, however fevere, to remain, but
boldly recovers its tempting fmoothnefs.
Next take a view of nature *centrally*;
no *folding lapel*, no *gaping orifice*, no
horrid gulph is here, but the *loving lips*
tenderly kifs each other, and fhelter
from the cold a fmall but eafily ftretched
paffage, whofe *depth* none but the *blind*
boy has liberty to *fathom* ; between the
tempting lips the *coral headed tip* ftands
centinal, fheltered by a *raven-coloured-*
bufh, and for one half guinea conduct
the *well erected friend* fafe into *port*.
She is a native of Oxfordfhire, and has
been a vifitor on the town about one
year, is generally to be met with at home
at every hour excepting ten at night, at
which time fhe vifits a favourite gentleman of the **Temple**.

Mifs

Mifs N—ble, No. 10, *Plough Court, Fetter Lane.*

She darted a fweet kifs,
The wanton prelude to a farther blifs ;
Such as might kindle frozen appetite,
And fire e'en wafted nature with delight.

She is really a fine girl, with a lovely fair complexion, a moft engaging behaviour and affable difpofition. She has a moft confummate fkill in reviving the dead ; for as fhe loves nothing but active life, fhe is happy when fhe can reftore it : and her tongue has a double charm, both when fpeaking and when filent ; for the tip of it, *properly applied*, can talk eloquently to the heart, whilft no found pervades the ear and fend fuch feelings to the central fpot, that immediately demands the more noble weapon to *clofe* the *melting fcene.*

Mifs Sophia M—rt—n, No. 11, *Stephen Street, Rathbone Place.*

Oh! the tranfporting joy !

Impetuous flood of long-expected rapture, fhe is a charming black beauty ; her vivid eyes, fpeak the livelinefs of her difpofition,

difpofition, and the joy fhe conceives in the hour of blifs. As yet fhe hath not approached the verge of fatiety ; fhe is not fo hackneyed in the ways of man as to be merely paffive, fhe enjoys the pleafure, and though fhe is very fond of a *noun fubftantive* that can *ftand* by itfelf, yet fhe loves to make it *fall*, and indeed the ftouteft man cannot *ftand* long before her ; many a *fine weapon* fhe has made a *mere banger* and the moft ftubborn fteel hath melted in her *fheath* ; yet no one complains, but rather rejoices at the debility fhe produces, and wifhes for repetition which fhe enjoys with a *gou* peculiar to herfelf, and is poffeffed of every *amorous* means to produce it, as fhe is of every lufcious one to deftroy it.—To be met with at any of the genteel houfes about St. James's.

Mifs W—d, at a Hair-dreffers, *Windmill ftreet, Tottenham Court Road.*

———— Fair

As May morning rifing from the eaft,
Or day difmounting from the golden weft.

This young charmer is of the middle fize, and the refplendent black of her
lively

lively eyes is finely contrasted by the fairness of her complexion and lightness of her hair : her teeth are good, and her temper complying. She is really a delicious piece, and her *terra incognita* is so very agreeable to every traveller therein, that it hath ceas'd to deserve that name, and is become a well known and much frequented country ; freely *taking in* the stranger, *raising* up them that *fall*, making the *crooked straight*, and although she does not pretend to restore sight to the blind, she'll place him in such a direction that he cannot mistake the way ; and for one guinea will engage he returns the same way back without any direction at all.

Miss Fanny C—rtn—y, *at Mrs.* Woods, *Lisle street, Leicester Fields.*

My heart's so full of joy,
That I could do some wild extravagance
Of love in public, and the foolish world,
That knows not tenderness, mig ht think
me mad.

This lady is fair, of a good size, very chatty, fond of obliging, and far from being mercenary : the more agreeable
her

her man, the lefs of money fhe expects
or demands. It is true, fhe has other
cuftomers that make up for what fhe
may loofe by her attachments to pleafure; fo that between the one and the
other, fhe is very well off, and we pro-
phefy will be long in vogue; we have
known her only fix months, and have
reafon to think very few has known her
longer.

Mifs R—fs, *at* Mrs. Wanpole's, No. 1,
Poland-ftreet.

Soft, as when the wooing dove,
  Woo's his mate in vernal bowr's,
Is this pureft child of love,
  When fhe her *choiceft treafure pours.*

Here youth and beauty are combined,
and unadorned by education or art; what
fhe *feels* in the *amorous encounter* cannot
be feigned. Her natural fimplicity is
yet fo unftained, and her knowledge of
the world fo very little, that it is almoft
impoffible for her to diffemble; her
hair, eye-brows and eyes, are of the
deepeft black; her complexion of the
rofes red, and her neck and breafts of
the

2

(35)

the pureſt white; her limbs are nobly
formed, every joint poſſeſſing the moſt
enchanting flexibility, which ſhe manages with uncommon dexterity, and her
Venus Mount is ſo *nobly fortified*, that ſhe
has no occaſion to dread the *fierceſt attack*, nor does ſhe: and although ſhe is
obliged to make ſudden *retreats*, her *ad-
vances* follow ſo very briſk, and are ſo
effectual, that

> Whene'er ſhe quits the field,
> Waits *vice* on her *lovely ſhield.*

but we muſt adviſe our lovers of the ſport
to keep her pleaſed, as her temper, a
little different from *another part*, is not
to be ſported with.

Miſs S—ms, No. 82, *Queen Ann's-ſtreet
Eaſt.*

> Like ſome fair flower, whoſe leaves all co-
> lours yield,
> And opening, is with rareſt odours fill'd;
> As lofty pines o'ertop the lowly reed,
> So does her graceful height moſt nymphs ex-
> ceed.

Miſs S—ms is fair and tall, and if
well paired, would be a very proper
mould

mould to caft grenadiers in ; fhe is about twenty, and though rather above the common heighth, is not ungraceful nor awkward. She knows her value, and will feldom accept of lefs than two guineas, which indeed, are well be-ftowed. It is remarkable, that her lovers are moft commonly of a diminutive fize. The vanity of furmounting fuch a fine tall woman, is, doubtlefs, an incentive to many, to fo unmatch themfelves, that they are content to be like a fweet-bread on a breaft of veal. Yet, notwithftand-ing her fize, we hear her *low countries* are far from being capacious, but like a well made boot, is drawn on the *leg* with fome difficulty, and *fits fo clofe*, as to give great pleafure to the wearer ; it is about two years fince her *boot* has been ac-cuftomed to wear legs in it, and though often *foaled*, (fold) yet never wears out.

Mifs B—lt—n, No. 14, *Lifle-Street*,
    Leicefter Fields.

Why fhould they e'er give me pain,
Who to give me joy difdain ;
All I afk of mortal man,
Is to ——— me whilft he can.

Thefe four lines were not more appli-cable to Mifs C—tl—y, than to this pre-
                fent

sent reigning lover of the sport; she is rather above mediocrity in height and size, with fine dark hair, and a pair of bewitching hazel eyes; very agreeable and loving, but she is not so unreasonable as to expect constancy; it is a weak unprofitable quality in a woman, and if she can persuade her husband or keeper that she has it, it is just the same as though she really possessed it. Miss B—lt—n is conscious she loves variety, as it conduces both to her pleasure and interest; and she gives each of her gallants the same liberty of conscience, therefore she never lessens the fill of joy, by any real or affected freaks of jealousy; when her lovers come to her, they are welcome, and they are equally so when they fly to another's arms. Indeed, when they do so, it is generally to her advantage, as she finds they return to her with redoubled ardour, and her charms are in general more dear, from a comparison with others; and although her age is bordering upon twenty-four, and she has been a traveller in our path four years, her desires are not the least abated, nor does she set less value on herself.

D   Miss

Miſs D-v-np-rt, No. 14, *Liſle-ſtreet,*
Leiceſter-fields.

The nymphs like Nereids round her couch
  -were plac'd,
Where ſhe another ſea-born Venus lay;
She lay and lean'd her cheek upon her hand,
And caſt a look ſo languiſhingly ſweet,
As if ſecure of all beholders hearts,
Neglecting ſhe could take 'em.

This young charmer, for ſhe is not
yet paſt the bloom of eighteen, has ſo
beautiful a face, that though here and
there the general ravager of beauty has
left his dented marks in a ſkin, that the
fineſt tints of the tulip, carnation, or
roſe, blended with the hue of the faireſt
lilly, cannot equal, (ſo vaſtly ſuperior is
the vermilion tinge of nature, in this her
choiceſt and moſt animated work over
all other) yet their effect is rather pleafing than otherwiſe; and perhaps have
tempered a blaze of beauty, which without them would have been inſupportable.
Her eyes are of that colour, which the
celebrated Fielding has given the heroine
of his moſt admirable work, and which
dart

dart a luftre peculiar to themfelves. From fuch an eye each look has power to raife

" The loofeft wifhes in the chafteft heart,"

and melt the foul to all the thrillings of unafked defire, till quite overpowered with the tranfporting gaze, the fenfes faint, and haften to enjoyment. Her hair is alfo black, of which great orna- ment, nature has been lavifhly bountiful, for when loofe, it flows in unlimited treffes down to her waift; nor are the *tendrills* of the *mofs covered grotto* thinner diftributed, but though not yet *bufhy*, might truly be ftiled *Black Heath*; how early this *thicket* of her maidenhead *was penetrated* through, by the natural *invader* of *Middlefex*, we cannot pretend to fay ; moft probably when it was only a fmall brake; for from its prefent ftate, and the extraordinary warmth of the foil, it muft have began to fhoot very early, and the mother of all things muft have opened the fanguinary fluices in this delightful *Channel*, at an early period. The mount above, has a moft delicious fwell, as ambitious to receive on it downy bed, its *fwelling rival* and

D 2 *antagonift*

antagonift, and it is fo well clothed, that
it may be juftly called the Cyprian
Grove; whilft her breafts are fo fine and
fo fully fhaped, as to entitle her to be
ftiled *en bon point*, in the richeft fenfe of
the words, and they have a fpringinnefs
that defies any weight whatever, of amorous preffure.   Here the voluptuary
might revel in pleafure, better imagined
than defcribed, in

" Soft filent rapture and extatic blifs,"

Her teeth are remarkably fine; fhe is
tall, and fo well proportioned (when you
examine her whole naked figure, which
fhe will permit you to do, if you perform Cytherean Rites like an able prieft)
that fhe might be taken for a fourth
Grace, or a breathing animated Venus
de Medicis.   Her difpofition and temper is remarkably good, fo fweet, that it
is your own fault if it be foured;
for fhe is poffeffed of an uncommon
fhare of politenefs, nothing rude or un-
courteous in her manner, but abounding
with civility and good breeding; her
connections are good, and fhe has a
keeper (a Mr. H—nn—h) both kind
and

and liberal; notwithſtanding which, ſhe
has no objection to two ſupernumerary
guineas.

Miſs G—rge, *at a Grocer's Shop, South
Molton-ſtreet.* №. 3 ?.

Haſt thou beheld a freſher, ſweeter nymph,
Such war of white and red upon her cheeks,
What ſtars do ſpangle, Heaven, with ſo much
   beauty,
As thoſe two eyes become that Heav'nly face.

At the tempting luſcious age of nineteen, this lovely girl preſents us with a
face well worth the attention of the *na-
turaliſt*; ſhe is of a fine fair complexion,
with light brown hair, which waves in
many a graceful ringlet, has good teeth,
and her tell-tale dark eyes, ſpeak indeed,
the tender language of love, and beam
unutterable ſoftneſs; ſhe is tall of ſtature,
and of the moſt tempting *en bon point*;
plump breaſts, which in whiteneſs ſur-
paſs the driven *ſnow*, and melt the moſt
ſnowy of mankind to rapture. Her name
ſhe borrows from a gentleman, who,
ſome little time ago, poſſeſſed her (as he
D 3   thought

(42)

thought) entirely for fome time, but finding himfelf miftaken, and tired with the
cornuted burthen on his brows, he left her
about fix months ago, to feek fupport in
this grand mart of pleafure; and as fhe
has been remarkably fuccefsful, and ftill
remains a favourite piece for the enjoyment of her charms, and the converfa-
tional intercourfe, with a temper remarkably good, for a whole night fhe expects five pounds five fhillings.

---

r.º 17 MifsC l—nt—n, *near Middlefex Hofpital.*

Mark my eyes, and as they languifh,
Read what your's have written there.

This is a very genteel made little gir,
with the languifhing eye of an Eloife;
like her too, fhe is warm with the *fire* of
love, in all its native freedom, which,
fanned by the amorous air, foon kindles
into a flame that cannot be quenched
but by the powerful effects of the
Cyprian Torrent, which fhe is very fond
of being *bathed in;* fhe has good teeth,
and a lilly white fkin, which is beautifully

fully contrasted by a *grot* black as the
footy raven, which, for two pounds two,
will entertain you a whole night.

Miss Betsy Cl—rke, No. 11, *Stephen-street*,
Rathbone Place.

Hope, with a gaudy prospect feeds the eye,
Soothe every sense, does with each with
comply;
But false enjoyment the kind guide destroys,
We lose the passion in the treacherous joys.

Enjoyment is the most exquisite of
human pleasures; ah! what a pity it is
so short in duration. Nature wound up
to the highest pitch, after striking *twelve*,
immediately descends to poor solitary
one: these are the reflections that na-
turally arise on enjoying Betsy. Though
she is but little, she is an epitome of delight, a quintescence of joy, which by the
most endearing chemistry, give all spirit,
and unite in small compass, the efficacy
of a much larger bulk. Her lovely fair
tresses and elegant countenance beat
alarms to love; but we attack only to
fall in the breach, and lament that the
luscious

(44)

lufcious conflict is fo foon ended. The common deftroyer of beauty has made a few dells on the face of this fair Jewefs, but a pair of pretty dimples makes ample amends, and quite over balances thefe trifling imperfections; fhe has been in life not more than fix months, and expects, if fhe calls any man a friend, to receive two guineas the firft vifit.

Mifs D—gl—fs, No. 1, *Poland-ftreet.*

See through the liquid eye, the melting glance,
The buried foul in lovely tumults loft,
And all the fenfes to the *centre fent.*

She is of the middle fize, light hair, blue eyes, and about twenty-two; fhe is a very agreeable companion, fings a good fong, and is a buxom, lively, lufcious bed-fellow, but has nothing remarkable above the common run of women of the town, who are young and handfome; fhe has been a fportfwoman in the Cyprian Games about five years, and always expects two pounds two before fhe is mounted.

Mifs

Miss Betſy H—ds—n, *at Mrs. Kelly's, Duke-ſtreet, Saint James's.*

How dull the ſpring of life would prove,
Without the kiſs that waits on love ;
From youthful lips you ſoon receive
The richeſt harveſt lips can give.

I: loped from her friends in the country
but a ſhort time, fluſhed with all the
amorous fire of youth inſatiate, and ripe
with every perſonal charm the heart of
man can wiſh, this pleaſing girl enters
our liſt. The freſh country bloom ſtill
remains unimpaired, the rural vivacity is
ſtill the ſame, and united with a beautiful ſkin and complexion, we can preſent
our readers with a temper and diſpoſition
that good nature and affability muſt call
their own. Her teeth are regular, and
very white, her eyes of the moſt lively
hazel, which, without the leaſt fire from
Bacchus, ſhoot the moſt powerful glances;
her hair a lovely brown, her breaſts are
ſmall and never have been ſufficiently
ſubjected to manual preſſure, to deprive
them of their natural firmneſs ; ſhe is
willingly compliant to any liberty in
company, that does not extend beyond
the bounds of decency ; but let nature
come

come forth *unadorned*, get once the
enchanting girl in bed, fhe *opens* all her
charms, and gives a fudden loofe to fuch
a bent of amorous paffion, fhe would fire
the moft torpid difpofition ; when once
you prefs her in your eager arms the
game muft inftantly begin, and fcarcely
does fhe allow an introductory kifs, fo
uncurbed is her appetite, and fo fond is
fhe of *repetition*, that fhe would wifh
every lover that paffes a night with her
to be able to fay with Ovid,

Fair Betfy knows, when numbering the delight
Not lefs than *nine* full tranfports crown'd the
night.

Only fix months has this child of love
dealed out her charms in public, but well
knowing their value, is not quite fatisfied
if fhe does not receive on *paper* a proof
of their excellence.

Mifs Br—wn, No. 8, *Caftle Street*, Ox-
ford Market.

Give me plenty of bub,
From the large brandy tub,
And i'll *fpend* the whole night in your arms,
I'll expofe every part
Of my brown *apple cart*,
And ftifle, quite ftifle the *boy* in its *charms.*

I hope none of our readers will prove a
Mr. L-d-tt, who, about fix months ago,
from

from a mere filly quarrel with this his favourite fair, thought it convenient to fin-
ifh, his exiftence in the *leaden way*; fhe
does not poffefs either youth or novelty
fufficient to tempt many, to act in that
way, having been at leaft feven years a
trading nymph to our knowledge; fhe is
tall, and genteelly made, with a fine fkin,
and beautiful flaxen hair, but is too fond
of the brandy bottle to give that fincere
delight, that *mutual interchange of fouls,*
fo neceffary to ftamp the *extatic rapture*;
fhe may, however, prove to thofe that
will drink a glafs with her, and has no
objection to become as merry as herfelf,
a defireable piece, as fhe is neither extravagant in her demands, or nice in the
choice of her admirers.

Mrs. D—f—ld, *at a Sadler's, Charles
Street, Soho.*

Then he began to rave and tear,
And fwore once more he'd try the fair
To grace his notes he would take care,
    She gave her kind confent.
He pitch'd the higheft note he could,
And kept the ftops juft where he fhould,
Damon, fays fhe, your mufick's good,
    And I am now content.

This lady, we are told, is remarkably
fond of mufick, and there is no *tune*
                                    within

within *compass of the flute* but she plays with the greatest dexterity; she is perfect mistress of all the *graces*, is never *out* in *stopping*, and is full as well skilled in *pricking*; altho' the principal part of her *music* is played in *duets*, and every *duet* in a *natural key*, she has not the smallest objection to *two flats*; she has a variety of sweet notes, and many pleasing *airs*, and generally chooses the lowest part; every *shake and quaver* she feels instinctively, and *sometimes* has played the same *tune* over *twice*, before her partner has gone through it once, without the least deviation from true concord; she does not allow of any *cross barrs*, and is particularly partial to the *Tacit* flute; her moving stars are as black and as round as the end of a *Crotchet*; no *flower that blows is like* her cheek, or *scatters such perfume* as her breath: no *advice can controul her love*; *she does as she will with her swain*, presses him *away to the copse*, puts the *wanton God where the bee ucks into her pleasant native plains*, soon after you feel the *graceful move* and find *how sweet* it is *in the low-lands*; and should it be *in sable-night*, *she loves to restore the drooping plant*, thinks *variety is charming*, and always *gives one kind kiss before she parts*;

and

and as she is now only nineteen, cán sing a French as well as an English song, and has a very good friend, whose name she at present assumes : you must not approach her shrine without being well fortifyed with *root of all evil*.

Mifs B—nd, No. 28; *Frith-ftreet.*

A rose-bud blows in either cheek,
    Round which the lily makes its bed ;
Two dimples sweet good nature speak,
    And auburn ringlets deck her head.
Her heaving breasts pant keen desire,
    Their blushing summits own the flame ;
Her eyes seem wishing *something nigher,*
    Her hand conducts it to the same.

Mifs B—nd is a very genteel agreeable little girl, and is diftinguifhed more by the elegancy of her drefs, than the beauty of her perfon, which might perhaps have been ranked in the lift of tolerable's, had not the small-pox been quite so unkind ; she is, neverthelefs, a defirable *well tem—*

E   *pered*

pered piece, and one that does not degrade herself by her company or her actions; she comes into our corps, in consequence of her good keeper's leaving England, and enlists a volunteer, in all the sprightlinefs and vivacity of nineteen, with beautiful auburn hair, and a pair of pretty languifhing blue peepers, that feem at every glance to tell you how nature ftands affected below; nor will thofe fwimming luminaries deceive you; *it* is ever ready to receive the *well formed tumid gueft,* and as the *external crura* entwine and prefs *home* the *vigorous tool,* the *internal crura* embrace it, and preffes out the laft *precious drops* of the *vital fluid,* which her hand, by ftealth, conveyed to the *treafure bags* of nature, by tender *fqueezings* feem to increafe the undifcribable rapture, at the *dye away moment;* in fhort, during her performance of *venereal rites,* fhe is all the heart of the moft inflamed fenfualift can wifh, or any man that has two fpare guineas in his pocket, can defire.

Mifs

Miſs Gr—n, No. 32, *Little Ruſſel-ſtreet.*

Strait a new heat return'd with his embrace,
Warmth to my blood and colour to my face ;
Till at the length, with mutual kiſſes fir'd,
To the laſt bliſs we eagerly aſpir'd,
And both alike attain'd, what both alike
            deſir'd.

When beauty beats up for recruits, he
muſt be an errant coward indeed, who re-
fuſes to enliſt under its banner; and
when good humour, complaiſance, and
engaging behaviour are the rewards of
ſervice, it is ſhameful to deſert. This
lady's charms attract moſt who behold
them; though of a low ſtature, and
rather under the middle ſize, ſhe is elegantly formed; her black eyes, contraſted
with her white teeth, are highly pleaſing,
and the goodneſs of her temper rivets the
chains which her agreeable form firſt put
on. One guinea, is then, too poor a re-
compence for ſuch merit; and it is to be
deplored, that a girl, who ſhould only
exchange love for love, ſhould be obliged
to take payment for what is ever beyond
price: in bed, ſhe is by far the better
            E 2   piece,

piece, and is up to every manœuvre
neceffary to reftore life, and every
lufcious *move* to deftroy; hands, tongue,
lips, legs, and every part of the bufy
frame is engaged at once in the pleafing
tafk, and all to provoke and bring the
foul breathing conflict to the laft *extatic
gufh.*

Mrs. D—d, No. 6, *Hind-court, Fleet
Street.*

——————————O my foul,
Whither, whither art thou flying,
Loft in fweet tumultuous dying?
You tremble love, and fo do I!
Ah! ftay, and we'll together dye;
My foul fhall take her flight with thine
Life diffolving in delight,
Heaving breafts and fwimming fight,
Faultering fpeech and gafping breath,
Symptoms of delicious death;
My foul is ready for the flight.

This lady appeared fome years ago, to
our readers, under the name of Ogl—,
but as we have frequently feen, that a
girl, though young, may yet be very
difagreeable,

(53)

disagreeable, so we may conclude, from Mrs. D—d, that a woman in years may be perfectly alluring; she is, indeed, turned of forty, rather fat and short, yet she looks well, dresses neat, and can divide as smartly covered, and as neat a leg and foot as ever beat time to *the silent flute*; her temper and behaviour are good, and if you are not soon disposed for the attack, she will shew you such a set of pictures, that very seldom fails to alarm the sleeping *member*. Then may you behold the *lovely fount* of delight, reared on two pillars of monumental alabaster; the symmetry of its parts, its *borders* enriched with *wavering tendrils*, its *ruby portals*, and the *tufted grove*, that crowns the summit of the mount, all join to invite the guest to enter. The cordial reception he meets therein, with the tide of *flowing bliss*, more delicious than the boasted nectar of the gods, engulph the raptured soul, and set the lovely owner of the premisses, above nine tenths of the green gewgaws that flutter about the town. If discipline forms the soldier in the wars of Mars, experience finishes the female combatant in the skirmishes of Venus. That experience this lady has, and is

E 3   per-

perfectly skilled in every delightful manœuvre, knowing how to keep time, when to advance and retreat, to face to the right or left, and when to *shower* down a whole *volley* of *love*; so that those who are vanquished by her glory in their defeat, pant only for returning vigour to renew the combat; she is perfectly mistress in the art of restoring life, and performs the tender friction with a hand soft as turtles down. Keeps the house, and after giving you a whole night's entertainment, is perfectly satisfyed, and will give you a comfortable cup of tea in the morning, for one pound one.

Miss Bl—ke, No. • 74, *Castle-street, Oxford Road.*

The soft desiring girl expects thy coming;
Busy in thought, and hasty for the hour,
She turns and sighs, and wishes, counts the
  . clock,
And every minute drags a heavy pace,
Till thou appear, the champion of the bed,
Arm'd at all points, and eager for the charge
That calls thee to the combat of thy love.

This lady's graceful figure, beautiful face, dark hair, and ivory teeth, must
                              surely

(55)

furely win the heart of every one, who
is fortunate enough to get into her company, and make you pant for the enjoyment of the more effential blifs; for
the performance of which, who indeed,
is better qualified? who is of a fweeter
temper? who can better twine in the enchanting folds of love? who can fill the
night with ftronger raptures? few, if
any. Inftead of expecting two guineas
for the performance, we may rather
wonder at her moderation in not expecting more : and though fhe is perfectly charming when dreft, yet we are
informed that her naked beauties are ftill
more enchanting; her lovely demi
globes of delight, with their ruby buds,
ravifh the wondering eye. Defcend ftill
lower to the *regions of happinefs,* the *true
country of pleafure,* and there appear the
flaxen tendrils wantonly playing over the
mother of all faints, whilft the *pouting
protuberances* leave it doubtful which *lips*
better deferve the burning kifs ; the extatic embrace both act in concert, and
charm with delightful unifon ; whilft
thofe *above* murmur the tranfports of the
foul, thofe which are placed *below,* perform the delicious fuction, which cannot
be refifted till every atom of the genial
juice

(56)

juice is drawn through its moſt natural
vent—that the man bleſt with enjoyment, may cry out with Lee, in his
Cæſar Borgia,

———— O thou great chemiſt, nature,
Who draw'ſt one ſpirit ſo divinely perfect,
Thou mak'ſt a dreg of all the world beſide.

Ireland lays claim to the honour of
giving birth to this charming girl, who
has not ſported her figure in public
life more than ten months; indeed her
particular friend, the Captain, whoſe
name ſhe has taken the liberty of
aſſuming, thinks her rather more honeſt
than we believe her to be; ſhe is now
in her eighteenth year, dances well,
and is fond of frequenting public hops,
where, if her partner pleaſes her, for
two guineas ſhe has no objection to
take him home, and return the compliment, that is, provided the Captain
is from town.

Miſs.

Mifs M—nt—n, No. 55, *Berwick-ftreet,*
Soho.

Toil all the night, and at the approach of
    morn,
When tir'd nature calls aloud for reft,
The wanton fair, a ftranger to fatigue,
With eager fondnefs will renew the fport;
Entwine the bufy limbs to force the joy,
Whilft through the parting lips, the playful
    tongue,
The vital fire thro' every nerve propels,
And drown the fenfes in love's potent ftream.

    Would the amorous *devotee* wifh us
to fay more, perhaps he may require
perfonal charms, even then he will not
be difappointed; fhe is of the brunette
caft, with fine languifhing eyes, fine
even teeth, plump, well formed, panting bubbies, and as fhe has now only
entered into her nineteenth year, cannot poffibly have loft the tranfports
of *mutuality*; at prefent fhe trades the
independant lafs, having no particular
                  friend

friend to humour or offend ; she takes
her noon and evening excursions re-
gularly, and enjoys, with unfeigned rapture, every man of pleasure that *enters* properly equipped for the sport ;
and her love of variety, and her attachment to the sport, is so very
prevalent, that, provided the gentleman's pocket is sufficiently armed,
there is not the least reason to fear she
then will meet him *midway*, with true
rapture, will *grasp* the *pointed weapon* with
genuine female fortitude, and urge him
home with singular delight, *lesson* his
pride with becoming dignity, and ask
repeated pleasures.————It is now only
eight months we have been able to
call her *our own*, and as she seems sa-
tisfied with one guinea, would recommend her as a *deserving* peice.

Miss K——n, *Castle-street, Oxford Market.*

" Let *Nature* empty her whole quiver in me,
" I have a *part*, which, like an ample shield,
" Can *take in al'*, and yet leave room for more.

This lady assumed the name, she at
present goes by, from motives of con-
cealment

cealment in her *sportive* profeſſion, in which ſhe drives a good trade, and is very much lik'd by the *beaux eſprits* of the age for her *ſpunk*, being remarkably full of Cyprian Spirit, many degrees above any proof it has ever been put to; ſo that for the power of her parts, and active ability, ſhe could match Turk Gregory; and when ſhe had him in her tenacious arms, he might perform the amorous feat within the *magic circle* of her charms, till even ſtrength, like his, was *ſpent*, and nature quite exhauſted of all her balmy ſtore, whilſt ſhe, untired, and ſpringing from the bed, would aſk a freſh attack, and ſtill give pleaſure in the warm embrace; ſhe is of a dark complexion, with a wide mouth, and extraordinary well formed for a winter's companion. She has no pretenſions to beauty, but founds her claims to public favour on internal merit, and her *capacity* and ſkill in the rites of Venus, appealing rather to the ſenſe of touch, than that of ſight; ſhe is in general to be met with at a favourite hop, at the weſt end of the town, and if Mr. B—rd ſhould not be there, you may gain the liberty of attending her home, and ſhe will thank you for half a guinea.

Mrs.

Mrs. H—rv—y, No. 21, *Queen Ann Street East.*

Behold thofe eyes that fwim in humid fires,
And trace her wanton thoughts and young
   defires;
Tafte thofe fweet lips, with balmy Nectar
   fraught,
And all the rich luxuriancy of thought:
Prefs her foft bofom—feat of fwelling joy,
Whofe charms invite the rofy pinion'd boy;
Who, fluttering here, may point the unerring
   dart,
Flafh in each eye, and revel in each heart,
Till bolder grown, your hand infatiate rove,
O'er her delightful *mount* and *fportive grove*;
Then all her limbs unbound, her girdle loofe,
There's nothing you can afk her, fhe'll refufe.

The above lines, from one of the
warmeft and moft elegant poets fancy
ever favoured, might be very juftly applied to this charming girl. Rich with
the glow of youth, and the charms of a
perfon, in which nature has been lavifhly
bountiful, fhe poffeffes a mind rarely,
very rarely met with in the frail
daughters of pleafure; generous, free-
hearted,

hearted, noble, feeling, and difinterefted, might appear to be too high founding epithets for a woman of this defcription. But however ftrange, it is not lefs ftrange than true; for fhe poffeffes qualities, which the want of, might make many a titled dame, poffeffed of that fingle virtue, or at leaft appearing to poffefs it) that fhe has unfortunately loft,—blufh, for they may all with the ftricteft truth be applied to her. Here then, may the man come, (nay, we advife him to) who wifhes in the morning, fucceeding a delicious night, to find his perfon and his purfe fafe, and his health uninjured; here may he come, and tafte every joy the moft lufcious defire can wifh; here may his very fenfe be fed, nor know fatiety, for joined to a beautiful face, an elegant form, and a graceful manner, you will find the agreeable companion, the good humoured girl, and the moft enchanting bedfellow; young, and not more than three months *on* the town, or *in* the town, fine hazel love-fwimming eyes, and dark brown hair, which left to twine in nature's wanton folds, plays loofely over a neck white as fnow unfunned, and fweetly fhades the moft enchanting *love billocks* nature ever planted

F   *below*

below, a jetty *black* furrounds the *pouting manfion,* rais'd on a pair of pillars that might *fhame* the *whiteft,* or mark the fmootheft alabafter, that twine in the amorous encounter, and feem to partake of that pleafure in the dye-away moment, that we cannot pretend to fet any value upon.

Mrs. Ch—fh—line, No. 36, *Titchfield Street.*

Reclin'd upon a couch the maiden lay,
And all her virgin charms expos'd to view ;
I faw them all, unfeen, and in her eyes
Read the mad language of untaught defire.

This Mrs. C—— may fay, when fhe firft feduced this *then* lovely girl from the boarding fchool, and taught her *willing* mind the ufe of that *machine,* her amorous defires fo ardently wifhed for.— She is the daughter of a banker in the city, and might have remained with her firft undoer for many years longer, had not her itch for *variety,* and the brandy bottle, got the better of every fub-fervience due to a keeper. Now arrived at the full age of twenty-fix, with fine

fparkling

sparkling blue eyes, genteel tall figure, her breasts rather full but not less firm, very fair, and contrasted beautifully by the blue branching veins which surround every part ; apparently light brown hair, but so covered with powder that the colour is doubtful ; of a sprightly and amorous disposition, and a very warm temper, especially when *tempered* by her favorite liquor, of which she loves to take large and copious libations, ever desirous of seeing the bottom. Her price is moderate, the smallest piece being as much as she in general expects.

Miss M—rr—s, No 59, *South Mortimer Street, Oxford Road.*

" Methinks I wish, and wish for what I know
  not,
" But still I wish,—yet, if I had that woman,-
" She I believe could tell me what I wish for.

Should the man of pleasure take a nocturnal ramble *into* this lady's lodgings, and be happy enough to find her at home and alone, he need not wish himself for that night under the influence of any other star than that of *Venus*; as she will

F. 2   very

very agreeably make the *dulest* hours to
pafs away with the foft mufic of love,
and beat time to its *filent* harmony in all
the luxury of foft delight ; fhe is of a
fine brunette complexion, hazel eyes,
which beam inexpreffibly fweet, remarkable fine teeth, plump firm bubbies, and
a ftately carriage ; fhe dances well, and
is amiable in her temper, lively in her
difpofition, and carries good-nature in all
her actions ; nor does fhe neglect any
thing in her power to pleafe her vifitors.
Her price is from two guineas upwards,
to any fum the gentleman fhe obliges
thinks fhe merits ; which at the blooming
age of twenty cannot be too much. Had
fhe lefs partiality for a certain hair dreffer,
we think fhe would be more pleafing to
the generality of her vifitors.

Mifs Elizabeth W—tk—ns, *Little
Chefterfield-ftreet.*

Love's fubtle fluid, and life's thrilling kifs
Glide thro' her frame, and fpeak the coming
blifs.

In this age of gallantry and pleafure,
when epicurifm is fo much practifed,
and

and variety fo much fought after, we are
happy in being able to ferve up a difh to
every palate, and here prefent our readers
with as delicious a one (that is when fhe
does not fmell of brandy) as would be
provided by the hand of luxury itfelf,
and ftimulate the moft languid appetite
to fall on with the greateft *gou* ; for in
Betfy is comprifed an epitome of delight,
rather above mediocrity in her fize, fine
dark eyes and hair, and a fine durable
complexion, and teeth that needs not the
dentift nor his dentrifice ; and a pair of
tempting full formed breafts, made for
the fwelling yielding joy, and to fend the
murmuring figh of rapture to the breathing trembling lip; and at the critical
juncture of fupreme pleafure, her whole
fpirit feems to diffolve within her, weep
thro' all her frame with exquifitely
thrilling languor, and *pour down* to
the *centrical point* from every Cyprian
fpring a whole *flood* of *liquid life* : for a
nocturnal bathe in this Cyprian fpring,
fhe expects at leaft two guineas.

F 3　　　　Mifs

Miſs Betſy R—l—ns, No. 12, *Little Titchfield Street.*

Juſt at fifteen the *down* of nature grew,
O'er the ſoft yielding *lips* of crimſon hue ;
The wanton fire of love began to play,
And on her boſom ſhew its powerful ſway ;
When two more years had ripened every joint,
All nature's power did to the *centre* point,

And ſtill continues to point there, never ſeeking for a more engaging part, than that whoſe natural inſtinct ſo forcibly point to that *central* abode ; and well may it point there, for ſhe can command a Paradiſe of bliſs ; a fair eye, and beautiful complexion, together with firm panting breaſts, buſy hand, which loves to be buſily employed in inviting the tumid gueſt to her dear land of delight ; the two grand ſupporters of which always unfold at the approach of this never unwelcome viſitor, whoſe *knocking* and entrance is generally performed at the ſame time ; the *dando* and *reddendo* game ſoon began, which cannot be won but by death. She is tall and genteelly formed, good teeth, a fair ſkin, and pretty melting light eyes, and was taught,
when

when in keeping by the furgeon fhe takes her name from, that kind of behaviour that does credit to herfelf, and is very rare to be met with amongft the frail daughters of pleafure.

Mrs. W———rd, No. 19, *Union Street, Middlefex Hofpital.*

There is a joy to melt in her embrace,
Diffolve in pleafures, not in delights.

She is a fine lufty well looking lady ; her eyes and hair are dark ; her teeth good, and her age about thirty ; fhe fees much company, and none depart unfatisfied, it being her ftudy to pleafe, and her pride to be thought worthy of a fecond vifit. She is very careful of her health, and where fhe has the leaft reafon to fufpect infection, is very ftrict in examining the ambaffador of love e'er fhe receives his tribute. Tho' a very generous dealer, and one who has dealt in our market at leaft ten years, fhe does not appear to be quite void of fenfibility ; but feems to give pleafing proofs that fhe feels delight, as well as beftows it. Her
old

old friend, whofe name fhe ftole, has been long dead, and by his death has reduced her to accept of almoft any fum her paramour offers. .

———————————

Mifs J—hn—t—n, No. 6, *Church Court, St. Martin's Lane.*

Here rofes red, and lilys fair,
The gifts of nature, deck her air.

Oh for a touch of the pencil of animation to color the picture of one of the moft lively productions in our exhibition; fhe is genteel and well made, with a beautiful face, the tints in which are done by nature alone, fine light hair, and a pretty leering eye, that would make a monk difregard his vow of celibacy, or a mahometan think that he had got one of the daughters of paradife; her mouth fmall, her lips tempting; her teeth even, white, and regular; her foot and leg fmart, and her drefs at once neat and genteel. But thefe are not the fole powers of this lady; fhe is acquainted at once

once with the whole rationale of love, as well as with the entire practice of it; and whether we talk of those mysteries which are only known by the adepts, or those more clumsily applied operations of the lower orders of the sisterhood, she is up to every thing in love's tactics. Her dialect does not tell us she is a native of Scotland, tho' her father, who is an half pay officer, yet resides there; at this period when the powers of love or lust are at their full bloom, necessity and inclination together, prompted her to become a dancer on our cyprian stage, and is very desirous of pleasing every man that makes her his partner, and is so very careful of her health, that before she receives her *guinea*, she must examine every *one* of her partner's *legs*.

Mrs. S--tt--n, No. 31, *Taviſtock-ſtreet.*

> When will the dear man come, that I may
>   hold him.
> Faſt as my love can make him, hug him cloſe;
> As my fond ſoul can wiſh; give all my breath
> In ſighs and kiſſes, tell I ſwoon with rapture.

All this she seems to say to each admirer; it cannot be true to all. But no,

no matter. Vanity whispers to each,
this is for thee alone, and the self-deceived
dolt believes it. Miss S—tt—n, indeed,
can give pleasure ; her agreeable person, animated eyes, and lively manner,
promise pleasing enjoyment, and in that
she does not deceive ; she artfully prolongs
the pleasure to its utmost limits, and even
then repines it is so short. She is of a
comfortable size, genteelly form'd, with a
pretty round face, a little pimpled, very
pretty orient teeth, and now just entered
her twenty-second year ; her lodgings are
neat and elegant, for the use of which,
and a little *black apartment,* she always
carries about her ; she expects, at least 3
guineas ; if not at home, in the evening,
is generally to be met with, in the green
boxes.

Miss C—p—r, at a China shop, *Russell
Court.*

Let me press therein my arms,
Tune of my heart, and charmer of my eyes,
Nay, thou shall hear the extacy from me,
I'll make thee smile with my extravagant passion.

This lady is neither handsome, well
dress'd, well lodg'd, nor well bred ; yet
she.

she will give more delight than moſt of
the finical dames, who think they do
their gallants a favour to admit their embraces at a high price. This humble girl
is thankful for a crown, and will teſtify
her gratitude in whatever way you chufe,
ſhe is willing to appear in the dreſs of
pure nature, as her ſkin is without ſpot
or blemiſh, her breaſts ſmall and plump,
and her limbs well turned and well proportioned. It is her joy to give joy, and
ſhe omits no means of procuring it;
though her compliance is ample, ſhe is
ſo reſerved in her demand that ſhe takes
what is given, and does not, like too
many of her ſiſterhood, ſeize the minute
juſt preceding the moment of extacy to
demand more, and either proceed or
draw back as her demands are gratify'd or
not. In ſhort ſhe is worthy of ſome degree of elevation, to enable her to walk
a more gainful round than Catherine-
ſtreet, or the Strand. She has lately been
to viſit her parents in Derbyſhire, and is
now returned a tolerable freſh piece
again.

Mrs.

Mrs. H—w—rd, No. 44, Moor's-place,
Lambeth.

Her brows are arch'd, and rather full and thin,
To shade the dazzling light that dwells therein.

Although Mrs. H—w—rd cannot be
more than twenty-six, she has been a true
sportswoman, at the cyprian games, for
at least twelve years, and has within these
late ones contracted such an habit of in-
timacy with the gin bottle, that unless a
person is particularly partial to it, it is almost intolerable, to approach her. At
Brighton, this last season, she was the favourite girl at Mrs. John—n's, and had she
not, through a foolish fondness, gave the
preference to her dear Mr. Sh—m,
it is in general believed Mr. W——, the
capital Brewer, would have taken her
under his own protection; she is rather too
short, and too fat, fine dark hair; and
eyes and eye-brows that answer very well
to her motto; the *grove* below is *well
thatched*, and ample enough in size to *take
in* any guest; but still she has learnt the
knack of *contracting* it, and a small made
gentleman may feel the tender friction.
When she elopes from her dear fellow,
she is to be met with at Mrs. J—nf—n's,
in German-street, and does not turn
away any money offered her.

Mrs. H—ll—ngb—rg, No. 4, *Castle-
Street, East.*

In hell and earth, and seas and heaven above'
Love conquers all, and we must yield to force.

This lady, tho' an adept in the art, so
nobly erases true impudence, with false
modesty, that her lover would be almost
lead to think his chosen fair, at first sight,
an immaculate Virgin. The *supreme gush*,
the enraptured moment she so mutually
interchanges, or at least seems so to do,
that she might well be stil'd the paragon
of her sex; and so perfectly well convinced of her own proficiency in the art,
(altho in spite, of those killing luminaries, embellished by a tolerable good
skin, she has too large a mouth ever to
be stil'd a beauty) she never will see her
man a second time, unless Plutus has sufficiently shewn his power first. Our
charmer was taken from her parents, and
taught the use of the *tree of life* at a very
early period; but never had the good fortune on her side to be much exalted : indeed, when we consider the more early
part of her life was spent, and the whole
of her education was received in a sea port
town, we cannot be much surprised.

G   Miss

Miſs R—b—nſ—n; No 14, *Liſle Street,*
Leciefter Fields.

Thou can'ſt not ſee one wrinkle in my brow,
My eyes tho' dark, are bright and quick in
turning,
My beauty as the ſpring does yearly grow,
My fleſh is ſoft and plump; my marrow
burning.

It is not ſurpriſing, the notice which
a lady, who as long *erected* her ſtandard
in the *field* of *pleaſure,* attracts from the
veterans in the ſame field. This is the caſe
of our heroine, now about twenty-eight
years of age, tall, rather luſty, and a
figure that ſpeaks true ſymmetry; handſome, a ſlight tinge of the brunette in
her complexion, with very fine dark hair,
fine hazel eyes, very dark, and finely
arch'd eye brows; indeed, ſhe has been
a very fine woman, and is far from being
in her wane of beauty; her hair, indeed,
is remarkably fine, and ſuch a length, as
to be able to be interwoven with her *once*
maidenhead thicket, now grown to a *fine*
buſhy arbour ſurtounding the *bliſsful cell* of
the blind ſovereign of wanton ſports,
where he reigns predominant over every
ſenſe,

fenfe, and fubjects all the reft to that of feeling ; here he keeps his court and holds his revels ; come then ye followers of Comus, plunge your burning *plough fhares* within the betwiching circle, and flake the hot breathing of untamed defire; here dance the round of joy till fenfe grows giddy in the maze, and tafte the delicious tranfports of maddening delight, till *panting nature ftriking the alarm*, proclaims a *dying paufe* to her own mufic, and *pours* forth the *flood* of mingled rapture; fhe has good breafts, and her limbs are finely turn'd and proportioned ; fhe is of a very good difpofition, and a moft agreeable companion, and is at prefent in keeping by a Mr. M—lls ; but being fond of the *glow* of youth, and the manly embrace of *full* vigour , fhe indulges variety, and is various in her expectation for fo doing

---

Mifs L—ndf—y, No 13, *Little Portland Street.*

What pity 'tis fo fine a face and form
Should fuffer pride, the cankerworms of joy,
That beauty to deform.

If a warm fon of Bacchus, flufh'd with the fullnefs of defire impetuous, would wifh

G 2   to

to melt a haughty temper down to the
ftandard of all complying love, let him
repair to this imperious golden hair'd
beauty, for however proud, fhe will ftoop
to conquer any bold *invader*; and you
may lay her on her back by clofing with
her in the athletic exercife of wreftling,
as fhe is very fond of Cupid's *hug*, and the
amorous *lock*, and will wait your *further*
attack with becoming fpirit, and engage
your *champion* of her *ring*, with a grafp,
till he is reduced to *bend* beneath the
powerful fqueeze, and *yield* all the *metal*
he has about him to his circling antagonift, who, fo far from behaving ungene-
rous, will give out in exchange as much,
or more rich treafure of another coin, in
token of mutual amity; in fhort fhe is as
fmart a little girl as you will in general
fee of her complexion and fize, and borrows her name from a gentleman who is
a very good friend, but does not expect
her to confine the whole of her favours to
him alone; but allows her to pick up her
odd guineas as fhe pleafes.

Mrs.

Mrs L—w—s, *Upper Charlotte Street,*
Rathbone Place. № 68.

Sure nature caſt one in her ſofteſt mould,
All mild and gentle, never made to ſcold.

Weſt Indies gave birth to this daughter of Momus by Venus ; the warmth of
the climebrought the charming girl's feeling to maturity at an early period, and
a gentleman, whoſe name ſhe aſſumes,
firſt *trod* down *Hymen's* fence, and made
her a perfect woman ; but the natural
warmth of her conſtitution ſoon compelled her to ſeek variety in our great mart ;
ſhe therefore left her good friend, and
now preſents the world with a ſweet
chearful diſpoſition, fine dark hair, and
eyes of the ſame friendly hue; fine teeth,
is ſhort and plump, and we have not had
her above eighteen months ; ſhe expects
three guineas for a whole night, but if you
make a ſhort viſit, one pound one ſhilling
is the leaſt.

Betſy

B—t---fy, *at Mrs.* Kelly's, *Duke ſtreet,
St. James's.*

—Endleſs joys are in that heaven of love,
A thouſand Cupids dance upon her ſmiles;
Young bathing graces wanton in her eyes,
Melt in her looks, and pant upon her breaſts;
Each word is gentle as a weſtern breeze
That fans the infant boſom of the ſpring,
And every ſigh more fragrant than the morn.

This beautiful girl, that goes by no
other name than Betſy, was formely a
retailer of apples, &c. She has lately,
with three other ladies, ſported her figure
at Bath, and was there the reigning toaſt
amongſt the firſt bucks of the place; ſhe
is delicately and genteely form'd, about
the middle ſize, very young and ſprightly, and modeſt in her converſation, except when proper occaſions demand wanton freedom; her hair and eyes are black,
and her teeth remarkably white, through
which ſhe plays the velvet tip with uncommon grace and ardour; we cannot
pretend to ſay who cropt the virgin bud
from the beautiful tree, but it could be
long before ſhe put herſelf under the care
and direction of Mrs. K——, and under
ſuch a tutoreſs we have no doubt but ſhe
will

will be foon fuch a complete miftrefs of
her bufinefs, that join'd with her perfonal
accomplifhments, will bring her into the
moft elevated life. Many of the poft
fteeds of Venus have been fo often hack'd,
that they are broken winded, halt in
their paces, and are well nigh founder'd,
fo as to be fcarce fit for any thing but
brood mares, if they are not too old.
There will therefore be full room for
Betfy to fucceed fome of the moft eminent,
as fhe is well worthy of the embraces of
the firft men in the kingdom. Some
who have poffefl'd her fpeak with raptures of the joy fhe beftows, they fay the
beauties fhe difplays when dreft, great
as they are, are trivial to thofe which cuftom keeps concealed; they fay the moffy
grot of Venus is perfectly enchanting ;
her thighs are two alabafter pillars,
which with the ebon tendril that play in
wanton ringlets round the grot, and
the crimfon lining of the elaftic portals,
form together that perfect *clare obfcure*, fo
much admir'd in painting, and which always produce a moft pleafing effect; that
her lovely fnowy breafts are quickly be-
fpread with purple meandring veins, and
that her murmurs, her broken fighs of
joy,

joy, and half fpoken words of delight in
the rapturous minute, juftify fully, the
exclamation of the poet.

> Oh! how fweet to fee her eyes
> Rolling in their humid fires,
> Where the nymph extended lies
> Full of love and foft defires ;
> Confcious red her cheeks o'er fpreading,
> And her heaving bofom rifing,
> Milky paths to raptures leading,
> Murmuring fighs her joys difguifing.

Mifs P—mbr—ke, No. 5, *Duke-ftreet, Adelphi.*

> Where did my foul in the dear tranfport go ?
> Did it with willing hafte to her depart ?
> It did, I'm fure, and fluttered around her
> heart ;
> It heav'd, it trembled, and it panted there,
> But all its weak efforts to ftay were vain,
> A kifs reftored the fugitive again ;
> My foul re-enterd, we repeated o'er
> A thoufand joys unknown to both before.

In the bloom of fixteen, tall and elegantly genteel, with fine black expreffive
eyes, and remarkable fine hair, which
flows

flows in graceful ringlets down her back, and with an envious fhade fweetly protects two of the moft enchanting fnowy hillocks nature ever formed. Mifs P——— may well pleafe, may well attract the eye. She does pleafe, fhe does attract, and upon every account well merits the attention of the man of true tafte. Untutored by art, and taught only by powerful nature, fhe charms in enjoyment; and as fhe has not, from over frequency, been rendered callous to the joys of love, fhe repays every rapture with intereft, and meets the blifsful moment with a tepid flood of delight. At prefent fhe is in good keeping by a citizen, not many miles from Fleet Market, and having been only three months under his care, has not yet been fufficiently broke for the fport, hope therefore that fome of our good friends will, by properly fupplying the citizen's place at thofe hours his employment obliges him to be abfent, *inftill* into *her* fuch *principles* that will at leaft raife her fpunk to *proof*; but altho' young, fhe can well difpenfe with a little more pocket money than her keeper allows, and always expects twice the number of pieces that her paramour gives proofs of his manhood.

Miſs Harriet Ll—d, *at a Toy Shop, German-Street*

——Born with every grace,
Ev'n envy muſt applaud ſo fair a face ;
Such is her form as painters when they ſhow
Their utmoſt art, on naked limbs beſtow.

This pretty little ſmart girl, this true
lover of the ſport, is at preſent in keeping
by a member of P.————t, not far
from St. James's ; but not being ſufficiently *membered* for her *lower houſe*, ſhe
appropriates the greateſt part of the
member's hard coin to ſupport and keep,
in good humour two favourites of her
own. The one a tender ſprig of the
law, the other a jolly hearty lookiⁿ
butcher ; but ſtill in ſpite of theſe three,
ſhe has her *beſt apartment* ready for any
one that is maſter of five guineas, and
will make her miſtreſs of the ſame ;
it is neatly ornamented with cheſnut
coloured fringe, is ſnug and warm, and
when not *too warm* (which we are told is
ſometimes the caſe) very comfortable ;
ſhe is now only ſeventeen, her dark eyes
have much luſtre and more meaning :
her

her limbs, tho' fmall, are well fhaped,
covered with a fkin fair as the fwan's
neck, and foft as its down, they are
perfectly pliable, and form a thoufand
true lovers knots, firft to facilitate the
entrance into her *apartment*, and then
to keep the enraptured lodger there as
long as poffible. Indeed, fhe never lets
one depart till he has paid his *rent* ; but
to fhew fhe is not avaricious, fhe
generally returns as much as fhe receives,
in the like *metal*, tho' not in the fame
coin.

Mifs Sarah S—dd—ns, *at a Hair-
dreffer's, Taviftock-row, Covent-garden.*

He dreffes her wig in a new fafhion way,
And black D—m—r as ufual is jovial and gay ;
She conftantly fmiles on her doating dear puff,
And thinks he can never be tumbled enough.

This good-natured piece of luxury
we have not been able to trace beyond
five years, at which time fhe made her
entry in no very high fphere, but meeting with great encouragement, fhe might
have done very well, but love, that
wicked deity, created for the ruin of his
female

female votaries, fhot poor Sally deep in
the heart ; going to partake of an
innocent amufement, vulgarly called
black bops, where twelve pence will gain
admiffion, fhe beheld, oh dire misfortune!
a lovely African, blooming with all the
hue of the warm country that gave him
birth, and fell at that inftant a facrifice
to the charms of the well made footy
frizeur ; for fome time fhe ranked him
amongft her own train, and charitably
exerted herfelf for his fupport, but
growing at length fatiated with his dear
company, and almoft ruined in the bargain, fhe difmiffed the gloomy object of
her late defires, and parted mutual
friends ; fince which time fhe has graced
the purlieus of Covent-Garden with her
prefence, and is perfectly well known
under the Piazza. She is about twenty-
three, light hair and eyes, a good fkin,
and fize compleatly adapted for this
feafon, and which feems to pleafe the
greateft part of her friends and cuftomers,
who think two arms full of joy *twice* as
good as one ; fhe is remarkably good-
natured and affable to thofe who favour
her with a vifit, and will take almoft
any fum rather than turn her vifitor
away ;

away; but if you abfolutely bilk her, beware of the confequence; for fhe is fo well convinced that fhe does not merit fuch treatment, that fhe will, if poffible, revenge the injury; but we hope none of our friends will ever pay her a whole nocturnal vifit without a fmall piece of gold in his pocket, as fhe is an able pafture maker, is up to every movement in the art of giving pleafure, and will oblige them in any way.

Mifs M—lt---n, No. 9, *Charles-ftreet, Covent-Garden.*

Here hafte ye gay, take pleafure on the wing,
Tafte all her fweets conjoin'd, nor fear her
fting.

This agreeable girl has a pretty face fuffufed with a good complexion, dark penetrating eyes, hair of the fame hue, which waves in gloffy ringlets o'er her fhoulders, a fet of good teeth, and a ftature of the exact medium between a giant and a pigmy; fhe has not been more than eight months in this grand mart of univerfal commerce, and now ftands out for a fettlement from fome of her *warm* admirers, which (being at the

H   rich

rich age of twenty, the prime of female charms, when every zeal that can enhance enjoyments is at its full zenith) she concludes ought to be a good one. Mr. N—by, a limb of the law, is her greateſt friend and her particular admirer, but does not ſeem to have any objection to her

"Flying abroad for food,"

and is not at all diſpleaſed to find her a guinea richer than when he left her.

Miſs Gr—ce, No 124, *Portland ſtreet.*

Forc'd to conſent, but never to obey,
Panting he lies; the *liquid minute* paſs'd,
She feedeth on the *ſtream* as on a prey,
And calls it heavenly moiſture.

Some ladies prefer the profit, others the pleaſure; ſome may divide it equally in their choice, and perhaps their may be, among Venus's tribe, the lady found almoſt indifferent to either; this lady however we may venture to affirm is not of the laſt ſtamp; ſhe is a fine inviting looking girl, with very lively Cupidinous eyes and a good complexion, and ſcarcely ever to be found but in a good humour;

and

and her paramour, provided he can prove himſelf the good bed fellow, has nothing to fear in this lady's company, as money with her is not the entire object, it is the enjoyment that conſtitutes her happineſs, and in that part ſhe is a truly lovely actreſs; her twining limbs never forget their office ; her buſy lips is miſtreſs of the genuine burning kiſs, and the intermediate parts move in every direction that can poſſibly enhance the coming joy, which ſhe will powerfully urge a repetition of, as long as dame nature can poſſibly afford it. She is at preſent in keeping by a French count, who though very jealous, often ſuffers her to ſport it in his chariot, during which time her telltale black eyes, is buſy in hunting for admirers, and can tip the wink and conduct him, if approved, to a ſafe harbour ; and altho' not ſo very fond of money, ſhe does not expect to have leſs than five guineas offered her.

Miſs

Miss M—l—sw—rth, No. 62, *Wells-street, Oxford-street.*

A summer's day will seem an hour but short,
Being wasted in such time-be guiling sport.

Without possessing any particular attracting charms this lady pleases, and has
many admirers. Her face is agreeable
without being pretty, she is well made,
without being strictly genteel; and a friend
to mirth and good humour, without vulgarity. She carries on a snug good trade,
without going much abroad, and is in bed
a very amorous companion. If she does go
abroad it is generally to some of the public hops, where she contrives to select out
her partner for the night, and will con-
vince him (although she dances well a-
midst twenty couple) that she *cuts* a much
better *figure* with only *one*, and being now
only twenty years of age, with good nature,
affability, and love depicted in all her
actions, no one that has three guineas in
his pocket, ought to be against parting
with two thirds to oblige her.

Miss

Miſs Betſy H—ſt—ng, No. 30, *Duke-ſtreet, St. James's.*

Bleſt with ſuch charms, the ſnowy heart could
    move
Such melting beauties ſovereign claims of love ;
She ſweetly ſmiles, unconſcious of her pow'r,
And with her pleaſing chat beguiles each hour.

It is an undoubted fact ſhe muſt
pleaſe, ſhe muſt charm the heart, and
win the ſoul to exquiſite delight ; how
can it be otherwiſe! behold her eyes,
drinking their living moiſture in cups of
the pureſt hazel, and holding converſe
with the heart, in ſuch a language, the
leaſt meeting glance muſt immediately underſtand ; behold her hair, gloſſy as the
pearly drops that gild the flow'ry field
when Phœbus firſt his eaſtern rays ex-
tends, and ſoft as turtles down ; which,
when ſuffered to ſport in nature's wanton
folds, hold all the graces in their ſportive
curls ; view next her teeth, as white as
the poliſh'd elephants, and beautiful as
white ;

Cheeks from whence the roſes ſeek their
    bloom,
And lips from whence the zephyrs ſteal perfume

but all theſe charms united, fall very
ſhort of her mental qualifications : her

H 3   lively

lively wit charms the heart, and makes
her the defirable companion; her behaviour, which in company never deviates
from the ſtrict line of modeſty, gains her
the trueſt merit : her apartments are very
genteel, and her dreſs correſponds with
her perſon. Her profeſſional abilities
are not leſs to be priz'd than her other natural gifts ; her natural ſtructure in thoſe
parts is ſo well adapted, that it muſt
pleaſe, and every additional improvement
to enhance the coming pleaſure our delicate charmer is well acquainted with;
being now only nineteen ſhe cannot, in
the leaſt, have loſt the keen edge of amorous tranſport ; neither are the eſſential
parts at all deprived of their magical
power; the liquid eye ſtreams with the
maddening fire of youth, with all the
deſires of unſatiated love ; the panting
heave, accompanying the quick interrupted ſigh, ſpeaks deſire in its fulleſt
tone; and ſo mutually does ſhe interchange the liquid ſtore at the die-away
convulſive moment, that all her ſoul ſeems
centred in the bliſsful ſpot. She is tall,
and elegantly form'd in every limb;
Mr. Arch—r, the muſician, is at preſent
her favourite man ; him ſhe will oblige
at any time, from every one elſe ſhe
expects three guineas.

Miſs

Miſs D—v—nſh—re, No. 9, *Queen Ann Street Eaſt.*

Fool ! not to know that love endures no tie,
And Jove but laughs at lovers perjury.

This lady is a native of Devonſhire, and has only been *one* of *us* four months ; ſhe is of a fine fair complexion, love tinctured cerulean eyes, fine teeth, and genteel good figure ; a charming partner in a dance, a very good companion by the fire ſide, and dearly loves an agreeable friend and a chearful glaſs ; many a *man* of war hath been her willing priſoner, and paid a proper ranſom ; her port is ſaid to be well guarded by a light brown *chevaux-de-freize*, and parted from *Bumbay* by a very ſmall pleaſant iſthmus. The entry is rather ſtraight ; but when once in, their is very good *riding* ; and when they have paid *port cuſtoms*, they are ſuffered to ſlip out very eaſily, though generally followed by a ſalute from *Crownpoint*, which haſtens their departure by cauſing the floodgates to open commodiouſly. She is ſo brave, that ſhe is ever ready for an engagement, cares not how ſoon ſhe comes to *cloſe quarters*, and loves to fight *yard arm* and *yard arm*, and
be

be brifkly *boarded*; fhe is beft pleafed
when her opponent is *well armed*, and
would defpife any warrior, who had not
two ftout *balls* to block up her *covered
way*, and did not carry *metal* enough to
leave *two pounds* behind him.

Mrs. N—t—n, No. 12, *Suffolk-ftreet,
Cavendifh-Square.*

The blooming looks of fpring, and'lovely red
As opening rofes, on her cheeks are fpread;
Her eyes that fparkle like the ftars above,
Appear the armory and throne of love,
Whilft thoufands of alluring graces wait,
And mingling charms form love's triumphant
    ftate,

This lady is tolerably handfome, with
a fine dark durable complexion, fine
hazel eyes and good teeth, which, by a
perpetual fmile, or rather grin, fhe has
acquired a very convenient knack of
fhewing ; fhe is tall, and the goodnefs of
her temper and difpofition render her a
very agreeable companion and makes
her at prefent much fought after. We
hear the firft toaft fhe drinks every day is
                                    to

to the health of Mr. N——, a gentleman of the law, whofe name fhe has
taken the liberty of fubftituting for her
own ; fhe has not yet been a year on the
town, yet has done great execution
amongft the tender hearts of the men of
the *ton,* many of which fhe has kindled
into a flame. She is as fond of variety
as any *baronet*'s lady, and will difplay her
naked beauties to any curious obferver,
without giving them the trouble to
mount on any other *man's fhoulder* to take
a peep at them. She is very tall, and
the *pit* in her black heath is faid to have
a confiderable profundity, and has baff-
led the art of many a gauger to take it
precifely with the beft dipping rules ; yet
though the attempt has been unfuccefsful,
it hath not been undelightful, for the
paffage being ftraight much pleafure has
been derived by the *gauger,* during which
pleafing paftime

A gentle warmth invades her glowing breaft,
And while fhe fondly gazes on thy face,
Ev'n thought is loft in exquifite delights ;

and fhe is fo generous, that as fhe knows
the hours of love are but fhort, fhe always
fills up every moment of them with rapture. She well knows how to wind the
clock

clock of nature up to the *higbeſt pitch*, and make the *human pendulum* vibrate to extaſy; nay, ſhe can ſo well fill up what the Poet calls the *dull pauſe of joy*, that its duration is ſcarce perceiv'd, and ſhe beats an almoſt inſtantaneous alarm to bliſsful repetition.

Miſs Br—wn, No. 5, *Glanville-Street, Rathbone-Place.*

——————————Sacrifice to her
'The precious hours, nor grudge with ſuch a
   mate
The ſummer's day to toy or winter's night.
Now claſp with dying fondneſs in your arms
Her yielding waiſt, now on her ſwelling breaſt
Recline your cheek, with eager kiſſes preſs
Her balmy lips, and drinking from her eyes
Reſiſtleſs love, the tender flame confeſs
Ineffable, but by the murmuring voice
Of genuine joy.

This lively girl is a native of Somerſet-ſhire, and being thought by her good parents the roſe of the garden, received an education perhaps beyond what their circumſtances would then admit of, and
                          pride

pride with innocence danced hand in hand. From a great defire of becoming well acquainted with the world fhe was apprenticed to a millener of the fame place,

Whofe parent *band* the firſt *ideas* form'd.

Scarce fifteen ripening autumns had arrived, e'er fhe felt the divine influence nature began to infpire her with; the little fluid nipples till now unnoticed and almoft unfeen, began to ftrut in all the elegance of infant prime; the heart began to feel their fovereign power, and modeft nature painted the budding blufh in the centre; nature's fink began no longer to be thought as fuch, fince now another fluid paffed the narrow bounds, and inftilled, by power inftinctive, frefh feeling into the whole channel, and every thought and every action feemed founded on thofe feelings. It is now about ten months fince fhe arrived, and enlifted in the Cyprian choir; fhe poffeffes a delicate fair complexion, with lively blue eyes, a pretty mouth, and is well embellifhed with two rows of polifhed ivory; we cannot pretend to ftile her a beauty, but her lively and chearful difpofition, and her accomplifhments

under

under *cover* in great measure compensate
for the deficiency in her person, and make
one pound one a trifle for a whole night's
possession.

Miss Ch—ld, No. 3, *Charles-Street,
Goodge-Street.*

To arms, to arms, the Cyprian Queen
Here braves the god of War,
And tho' on back, not backward seen
To take his wond'rous spear,
And melt it in her *clasping fold,*
The fold of rapturous burning bliss,
'Till quite o'erspent in nature's *mould,*
Then darts fresh vigor with a kiss.

If a first rate smart little buck would
wish for a mould to cast light infantry
men in, we would strongly recommend
him to Miss Ch—ld. She has a noble
martial disposition, and would sooner die
than be out rivalled ; but independant of
that occurrence in her professional line,
her temper and disposition are good, and
her abilities between the sheets are not
easily equalled, excelled they cannot be ;
she

she poffeffes a pair of love fpeaking cerulean eyes, and a bofom as rich with love's
choiceft graces as luxuriant fancy can
paint, and filled with the moft irreftable
firmnefs, whofe panting redundancy foon
invite the amorous encounter, and calls
into action the till now *hidden friend*,
whofe fwelling pride and impertinence
will no longer fuffer the curtain to remain
drawn. She may, perhaps, at firft attempt
to chide, but bolt the door, and then all
chiding ceafes; an experienced fofa
then lends its aid; her turning limbs enhance the *coming pleafure*, and fighing
kiffes crown the *golden minute*; her fair
complexion charms the heart; her wicked blue eyes enchant the foul; her well
made form tempts the touch; her lovely
voice charms the ear, and her gloffy flaxen
hair is worth a guinea an hour to look at.

Mifs T—wnsd—n, No. 23, *Ruffel ftreet,*
Covent Garden,

Give me but thee, I'd make a heaven of earth,
Each night fhould give to new born pleafure
  birth;
The fun of *joy* fhould point continual *noon*,
And e'er an age of Noah, pafs too foon.

Thus fung prince ———, when he
firft became bewitched with the dancing
I   and

and finging of this fprightly piece, and
in confequence placed her in a genteel
lodgings, and for fome time was, we believe, her fole enjoyer ; but with all his bewitching power, his fhow of arms, his
awful countenance; his martial figure,
and his warlike voice, could not confine
this amorous virago within the bands of
conftancy, on whioh account it is in general believed he left her, and now fhe
trades the independant woman. Her
beautiful complexion and her fine blue
eyes open fuch a field for love, that whilft
they retain their prefent luftre, fhe cannot
be without admirers. Her fhape is elegant, her ftature tall and genteel, and
taking he revery feature conjunctively, we
may fay with the poet

Here youth and beauty, dancing in her hand,
Perform their myftic round of amorous joy,

She is now in her eighteenth year, and has
only been engaged in our bufinefs ten
months, and tho' fhe cannot be ftiled an
epicure, fhe is moft undoubtedly a glutton, being particularly partial to that meal
where *four haunches* are ferved up at once :
in her company they are fure to be drefs'd
in tafte, for fhe always chufes to *fpit* them
herfelf ; and always has the greateft

fhare

(99)

ſhare in *preparing* the *ſauce* ; her price for turning *cook* is at leaſt three guineas.

Miſs Fr—ſ—r, *Charlotte ſtreet, Rathbone Place*.

Not leſs her blandiſhments than beauty move
At once both giving and confeſſing love.

This lady is about twenty-five, very ſhort, with dark hair and black eyes; and was it not for her noſe, which is quite of the pug caſt, we might ſtile her a compleat black beauty ; her *toute enſemble* is very agreeable, and her blandiſhments make her a deſirable companion, as ſhe dreſſes in the height of the *ton*, ſports an elegant *rattler*, and at preſent figures away in the firſt line. She has got a ſmattering of the French and Italian (from which laſt place ſhe is lately come over,) where we are told a prince of the blood took particular notice of her, and learnt her muſick and dancing ; it is about ten months ſince we have been able to preſent her to our readers, and if you ſleep a night with her, not leſs than half the number of guineas will ſatisfy.

I 2   Miſs

Mrs. W—d, No 3, *Lifle-ftreet*, *Leicefter Fields*.

Oh ! that deceit fhould fteal fuch gentle fhapet,
And with a virtuous vizard hide deep vice.

Mens palates are as various as their
faces, and like a good ordinary we would
offer up a difh for every palate.   In the
time of the ancient Romans we are told
that the fat paps of the fow where held a
great dainty.   For thofe that have a re-
lifh for fuch a repaft we recommend
Mrs. Wood, and can affure them, fuch
paps as fhe poffeffes are feldom to be met
with.   She keeps the houfe, and is wife
to 'fquire P—'s coachman, late of the fta-
bles, Bolton ftreet ; her front is well bra-
zen'd ; her face is continually upon the
full grin, and as for talking bawdy, fwea-
ring, or bare fac'd indecency, fhe could
vie with the ancient *Mefelina* of Rome;
fhe difpenfes her favours for any fum to
one whofe arms are fufficiently long to
embrace her, and may do now, but in
the dog days muft be intolerable.

Mifs

Miss J—nes, No. 75, *Newman-Street*,
Oxford-Street.

————Oh she's all softness,
All melting mild, and calm as a rock'd infant;
Nor can you wake her into cries, by heaven!
She's the child of love, and she was born in
smiles.

Oh may the giddy rake, whose head
overpowered by the effects of the grape,
whose every thought, whose every idea
lies centered in the gratification of a
sensual appetite; whose impetuosity in-
discriminately rushes him on the first
object that presents herself, may he, at
this his most unguarded hour, rest in the
arms of this enchanting girl, whose good
nature, care, and attention, might make
him reflect with pleasure on the past
folly. In her he'll meet with every
pleasing accomplishment the heart of
man could wish; her natural disposition
as yet remains unvitiated by the knowledge
of the world, or corrupted by the hand
of time. She is now in her eighteenth
year, with every amorous feeling nature
at this youthful period can furnish her
with; nor is she desirous of keeping
those feelings a secret. Look in those

I 3   fine

fine black eyes, there read the perfect
language of her foul, for never was
filent language fo fully feen and felt ; fhe
has a fine open handfome countenance,
tall of ftature, and if her man is pleafed
with a good fong, he won't be difappointed by putting the requeft to our fweet
J—nes, whofe good nature is fuch fhe
never refufes,

> Or fhould he wifh to join the merry dance,
> Where the brifk couplets artfully advance.

Here likewife with our charmer as a
partner would he be equally delighted;
here fhe difplays fuch a leg and foot, and
with fo much activity, fprightlinefs, and
judgment, that none can fee but admire,
admire but love ; with all thefe qualifications, fay you, fhe cannot be a bad
bedfellow ; fhe has equal merits in bed,
and pleafes there with equal certainty.
She is neither covetous, nor will fhe
fink below what her real merits deferve ;
if after this, and our readers recollecting
fhe is but lately arrived from the lewd
mountains of Wales, he thinks two
guineas to much, he had better fteer fome
other courfe.

Mifs

Miss Charlotte C—sd—l, No. 25,
Titchfield Street, Oxford-Street.

'Till haply wandering in the fields of air,
Some fiend had whisper'd C—sd--l, thou art
fair.

We cannot help thinking but this was
the case with our charmer in question ;
who, as we have heard, felt her first
desire for the sport from meer inclination ;
she is tall and genteely framed, a pretty
innocent looking face, and a pair of
tempting breasts, that nineteen blooming
autumns have brought to full maturity ;
a lively blue eye and flaxen hair ; a
pretty reserved manner, (excepting when
exhilirated by the chearful glass) which
adds a particular grace to every feature,
and makes her doubly pleasing, fully
verifying Dr. Amstrong,

The coyley yielded kiss charms most,
And gives the most sincere delight ;

Cheapness offends.

Her temper is sweet, her manners affable,
and her disposition good. She is remarkably fond of dancing, and on that
account frequents most of the public
hops ; where she generally picks up her
spark, which is no longer a spark for her,

if

if he is obliged to change the laſt guinea
to pay for coach hire.

———————

Miſs C———p, No. 2, *York-Street,*
Middleſex-Hoſpital.

Give me a nymph with all her charms,
A full grown nymph to fill my arms ;
And leave to them that cannot feel,
The inſipid things they call genteel.

Strange it is, but not leſs ſtrange than
true, that Engliſhmen in general have a
great itch for variety ; and according to
our promiſſary note in the preface, we
here preſent them with one of the fineſt,
fatteſt figures as fully finiſhed for fun
and frolick as fertile fancy ever formed ;
fraught with every melting charm that
can be found in the field of Venus, fortunate for the true lovers of fat, ſhould
fate throw them into the poſſeſſion of
ſuch full grown beauties. Can you
conceive the lighteſt tints of an Italian
ſky ? ſuch then her melting eye ; can
you figure to your imagination the ſwelling ripeneſs of two tempting cherries?
ſuch

fuch then her lips; though fome might
be led to imagine if they were a fize lefs,
they would be full as tempting. Can you
place before your eyes, two beds of down
for Cupids to fport on? fuch then her
breafts. Would you wifh for an *ambufh*,
for fome of their more wanton brothers
to play at *hide* and *feek* in? fhow them
her Cyprian mounts. Have you a defire
to roll in the loofe lufcious lap of lip-
inviting luxury? *fpend* an hour in her
arms; that is, if Mr. C—tt—n fhould
not be there firft; he being fo great a
favourite, fhe is always denied when in
his company. If not at home, fhe is to
be found at any of the public hops, and
in general with her favourite man, who
we are told, won her firft by virtue of his
fiddle-ftick, and has, fince her firft attachment, kept her in very good tune; if any
of our readers wifhes to try a tune with
her, *he* mùft pay for it; but fhe is not at
all exorbitant in her demands, feldom
wifhing to turn money away.

Mifs

Miſs Nancy D—v—s, No. 31, *Well's-ſtreet.*

Well pleas'd at the *frolic*, ſhe laugh'd at the
    pain,   •
And wiſh'd with more ardour, to try it again;
Which, when *handled* and *dandled*, and made
    fit for uſe,
She puſh'd with leſs pain, as the parts grew
    more looſe;
Then *upping* and *downing*, kind nature told
    how,
She cry'd over-raptur'd, it does not hurt now.

This was her confeſſion to her dear Mr.
Wh—te, had ſhe leſs partiality for him,
her friends in general would have a greater
partiality for her; ſhe has a tolerable pretty
mouth, we wiſh we could pay her teeth
the ſame compliment; that mouth ſhe
thinks ſerves as an index to its *couſin below*; to be ſure ſhe has learned the wrig-
ling part of pleaſing, and would willingly make her gentlemen believe, when in
the *heat* of the engagement, that he is
giving her pain; but however large the
premiſes may be, ſhe certainly has attained
a very pleaſing method of *contracting them*,
never meeting with one ſhe could not perfectly well accommodate, from an infant
                                        ſhoe

ſhoe to a *jack* boot. She is of the middling ſize, with dark hair and eyes; retains a good complexion without the aſſiſtance of rouge or pearl powder; is very lively and chearful, and as a converſation piece only, would make the time paſs away agreeable enough, being chearful and good humoured, with a pleaſant ſmile upon her countenance; will drink a chearful glaſs to George the third with pleaſure, and whilſt ſhe has the glaſs in one hand, has no objection to ſee his picture in the other; but ſooner than her dear man ſhould want, ſhe would retail Her charms at five ſhillings an hour all day long.

Miſs K—lp—n.

Thoſe formal lovers be for ever curſt,
Who fetter'd free-born love with honour firſt;
Who through fantaſtic laws, are virtue's fools,
And againſt nature, will be ſlaves to rules.

We cannot pretend to ſay where this curious oddity lives, that being a circumſtance ſhe carefully conceals; and what is more extraordinary, ſhe never can be prevailed on to go into taverns or other houſes with a gentleman. To
what

what purpofe then (fome reader may fay)
is fhe inferted here, if fhe will not go
into a houfe to difpenfe her favors, nor
is it known where fhe is to be found ? A
little patience, good fir, and you will be
informed where fhe is to be found, and
how to procure her favours. If you
walk on the right hand fide of the way,
from the corner of Cheapfide along St.
Paul's Church-Yard, and thence to the
bottom of Ludgate-Hill, juft after fun-
fet, and meet wirh a beautiful woman
about twenty, tall and finely fhaped,
with fine black eyes, and hair of the fame
hue, that floats in curls down her back,
and worn without powder, and a bewitching dimple in each cheek, you may
give a fhrewd guefs you have found Mifs
K—lp—n. Her drefs is in general filk,
fometimes a pale blue, but oftener a
black, and a large white fattin cloak,
trimmed and lined with rich brown fur;
her head is in general bedecked with a
blue beaver, with a profufion of white
feathers; and if on accofting her, you
are as much dazzled with her wit, her
fmart repartees, and her delicate agreeable raillery, as with her perfon and
drefs, you may be then abfolutely certain
it is the lady.——But you may fay, when
found,

found, of what fervice is it, when fhe
will neither take you home with her,
nor go into any houfe with you ? A little
more patience, fir, if you pleafe, though
fhe refufes to go into any *houfe* with you,
are there not hackney coaches on every
ftand ? we have not faid fhe will deny
entering one of them with you; that is
if fhe likes your perfon and converfation.
And here let us add, no frothy coxcomb,
no male adonis, conceited of his own
dear perfon, no fhoe ftringed effeminate
puppy, no infipid empty chatterer, can
hope to fucceed with her.

If, reader, thou art neither of thefe,
and fhould meet with, and pleafe Mifs
K—lp—n, fhe will take as length'ned
a ride with you as you pleafe; and if
you have the prudence to draw up the
blinds, fhe will be as free as you pleafe,
and you may enjoy her charms, *Jehu* like,
as long as you can. She is framed for
love, and will melt like a fnow ball in the
fun. She will embrace you with unfeigned rapture, open *all* her charms to
receive your manly tribute, and perhaps
appoint another meeting.

We have rather enlarged on this lady,
on account of the fingularity of her difpofition; and what will add to your won-

K   der

der is, that she never will receive any
money, but take the offer as an affront.
These circumstances make us conclude
that K—lp—n, the name she has assumed
sometimes, is not her real name, and
that she is not a woman of the town, but
some married city lady, who takes this
method of getting home deficiencies supplied abroad, and, as she is cautious of
her character, uses these precautions.
By not going to any house, she avoids
detection; by chusing none but those
whose conversation is congenial to her
own, she obliges none but men of sense
and honour; and by her constantly re-
fusing money, she demonstrates that love
for love is her motto; that her love of
the sport is her motive; perhaps she
may have another reason for chusing a
leathern conveniency as the scene of her
delights. We have been told that the
undulating motion of the coach, with
the pretty little occasional jolts, contribute greatly to enhance the pleasure
of the critical moment, if all matters are
rightly placed. This she may have experienced, and therefore as pleasure is
her search, no wonder she prefers every
delicate addition to the grofs sum.

Emma,

Emma, *at Mother Gray's*, No. 30, *Market-Lane, near the Opera House.*

In the middle of me,
You plainly may fee,
A thing that will fuit every man ;
And when you are in it,
The critical minute,
Enfure as faft as you can.

A young tit of Mother Gr—y's own
procuring, and that our reader fhould
not miftake the old abbefs, we will give
a fhort defcription of her. If you chance
to vifit her in the morning, the fmell of
yellow ufquebaugh will falute your nof-
trils, of which fhe takes copious draughts
before breakfaft. In all her actions fhe
fhews the lewdnefs of a monkey, and
the letchery of a goat ; fhe has lately
been *fired* by P———, the French frizeur, but knowing the ufe of murcury,
fhe applied it in fuch a manner that fhe
procured an effectual falivation, and
enabled her to take into her houfe the
fame fquinting gentleman that prefent
acts as her *fine man* ; fhe boafts of her
knowledge of great men, and there is
fcarce a lord or duke in the land that
has not been her *cull.*

We

We can but pity our little girl in queſtion for being ſo unhappily ſituated; ſhe is a charming ſprightly laſs, and ſo fond of kiſſing, and ſo perfect a miſtreſs in the art, that ſhe will frequently force nature to a diſſolving pitch, before the *right parts* come in proper contract; her livelineſs of diſpoſition, and activity in the ſports of Venus, make her ſo deſirable a bed-fellow, that her magic *ring* is as much ſought after as the philoſopher's ſtone; has good hair and teeth, a plump round firm breaſt, and confined merely as an object to ſenſual deſire, poſſeſſes every qualification a ſenſualiſt can deſire. She is to be met with every night at Sterling's, and being newly come on the town, and poſſeſſing too much innocence, as well as ignorance, to fight the world as ſhe ought, ſhe is frequently bilked; but this there is no doubt ſhe will ſoon get the better off, particularly if ſhe follows the precepts and advice of the old lady ſhe lives with.

Miſs

Mifs Phœbe B—rn, No. 5, *Eagle-
ftreet, Red Lion Square.*

Behold her round the vine, in loofe attire,
Her panting bofom thrills with foft defire,
Which white and firm invites the amorous hand,
And never fails to make the member ftand ;
Then to her couch fhe'll lead the conquered
  boy,
Who in her feels a tickling pinching joy.

Bifhopfgate-ftreet is the place that gave
birth to this volatile charmer; her father
moved in the fphere of a hackney-coach-
man, and reared this daughter of Venus
with no fmall care, till fhe attained her
fixteenth year, at which period, a young
man about twenty wooed her, and fhe did
not repulfe him; but found his embraces
fo agreeable, that fhe foon wifhed for
food more fubftantial than kiffes; but
then the thought of facrificing her character to her pleafure was a bar not eafily
furmounted, but nature called fo loud
for its favorite *choak pear*, that fhe refolved
to throw herfelf into the arms of the
vigorous youth, and for the firft time

K 3   fuck

fuck the juice of the enchanting fruit ;
a few promises and vows of his, fully
preponderated all her maiden niceties,
and she soon yielded to the giddy im-
pulse of her passion ;

> She did not stay for marriage, that stale
>
> trick,
>
> But lost her reputation for a ———— ;

but the cruel laceration that this first
attack was productive of, obliged her to
confine herself to her bed two days, and
led her parents to the discovery of their
daughter's shame, which so highly in-
censed them, that they abandoned her to
the world at large ; and from this æra
we may date her entrance into life. The
Kite, in *Catherine-street*, first *scooped* upon
her, and carried her to the *nest* as a fine
prey, and she was not mistaken; she
proved such, and for six months never
was in want of *culls* ; at the end of this
time she deserted the mother abbess,
took apartments in Glanville-street, and
traded on her own *bottom*, where she
figured away with tolerable grace for
three months, and then removed to her
present situation. She is diminitive in

size,

size, with fine black eyes, large firm, and full breasts, a handsome mouth, pretty curling brown ringlets, and delicate little hands ; a very pretty leg and foot, which is at all times ready to divide and *house* its old friend, at the very low price of one ounce of silver.

Miss Charlotte C—tt—n, N●. 34, *King-street, Soho.*

———The self same cates
Still offer'd, soon the appetite offend ;
The most delicious soonest.

How happy would it be for the author of this anniversary publication, could he procure a friend to new christen the features, that the reader might with less fatigue go through this heap of tautology, but as that end is not yet accomplished, we must steer according to the old line,

An eye must still be an eye, and a tooth a tooth ;

both of which our young Venus, who has just reached her seventeenth year, possesses in a superlative degree. She strongly points to your imagination a casket of
orient

orient pearls, the former of two living diamonds, whofe language fo forcibly invite
the blind boy to the happy cloyfter, that
there is feldom many fleeting moments
before an almoft involuntary attack muft
be made. Her heaving breafts foretell
the *coming* joy ; the *liquid eye* declares it
nearer ftill ; the *interrupted figh*, the fudden *gufh*, if preffure and *involuntary twift*
of the limbs fpeaks a *flowing* of the *tide*,
and the critical oh ! bids the filly pen
defiance to exprefs. She is of a good fize,
and well form'd, of a lively and fweet
difpofition, has been but a fhort time in
life, and has beautiful dark hair ;

> Her eye brows arch'd, and rather full than
> thin,
> To fhade the dazzling light that dwells within.

She has met with many admirers, but
fhowing lately too great a partiality for
the gentleman whofe name fhe affumes,
(a horfe jockey) fhe has lately funk a
little in the world ; his late inconftancy,
however, has wrought fo powerfully upon
her, that fhe is now foliciting the favours and fupport of her old friends ; fhe
is of a good fize, and well made, of a
lively and fweet difpofition ; loves a glafs
of Madeira, but never takes a glafs in
one

one hand without having prudence in
the other, and is particularly careful that
the effects of Bacchus shall not prevent
the more sensible joys of Venus. Two
pounds two shillings is her price to stran-
gers, but if a very old and good acquaintance, she will not refuse half the sum.

Miss Cl—rk, No. 116, *Wardour-street.*

If any wench Venus's girdle wears,
    Altho' she be ever so ugly,
Roses and lilys will quickly appear,
    And her face look wond'rous smugly.

In some respect Miss C—— verifies
this remark of Mr. Gay, for very little
else than her wearing Venus's girdle can
invite any to admire so plain a countenance; she is tall and lusty, with dark
hair and eyes, a very indifferent set of
teeth, and a very flat face; she is now
twenty-five, has followed the trade some
years, and never refuses any sum scarce
that is offered her.

Miss

(118)

Miſs W—ls—n, No 1, *Little-court,*
Caſtle-ſtreet, Leiceſter fields.

Nature for meat and drink provides a place,
And when receiv'd they fill their certain ſpace;
Hence *thirſt* and *hunger* may be ſatisfy'd,
But this repletion is to love deny'd.

This pretty piece of animation wants
not the aid of art to make her ſhine one
of the moſt conſpicuous in the liſt of trading nymphs; altho' ſhe cannot be called
very handſome, ſtill ſhe is a fine girl,
and nature has ſufficiently furniſh'd her
with thoſe beauties the niceſt hand of
art would only deface. Her want of
pride (which is in this age a very rare
perfection) ſets off to ſuperior advantage
every feature; her goodneſs of temper
and diſpoſition acts as a ſecurity to her
moſt valuable acquaintance, and her juſt-
neſs of principle gains her the eſteem of
all who have the happineſs of knowing
her. She is the daughter of a gentleman
who holds a conſiderable place under
government, has had a genteel education,
and ſeems quite untainted with the vices
of the town; her great attachment to Mr.
J—n, of the theatre, is a bar to her ſeeing much company; with them that has
the good fortune to ſleep with her, will find
ſhe

she still enjoys the pleasure without the least satiety; no licenc'd fair during the honey moon can charm with more rapture, or feel the poignant bliss with more extacy; every inviting motion is us'd, every limb employ'd, to make the dying transports meet. Her own home is the place where she in general sees her company, and every visitor that passes the night in her arms, she expects will make her two guineas richer.

Mrs. Eliza W—bst—r, No. 13, *John-Street, Tottenham-Court-Road.*

Fancy itself, e'en in enjoyment, is
But a dumb judge, and cannot tell its bliss.

Mrs. W—bst—r is the daughter of a gentleman, deceased, has received a good education, which she improves by an excellent natural understanding; her age is twenty-one, her figure tall, and every limb elegantly proportioned; she possesses an agreeable face, but we will not flatter her by calling it a pretty one, being too thinly formed to constitute beauty, and too much pitted with the small pox to be stiled handsome; still she commands

commands a beautiful pair of dark eyes,
which give a moft pleafing, amorous
expreffion to her whole countenance, and
makes her, tho' not a pretty, ftill a very
defirable girl; fhe poffeffes a lively and
entertaining manner, with an affable difpofition, and refined delicate fentiments,
which has lately very much been abufed
by the brutality of her late keeper, Mr.
K—d, well known at Garraway's cof-
fee houfe, for the lownefs of his birth,
and ftill greater meannefs of his fentiments. He was fome time fince a corn-
factor, but has now relinquifhed that,
and now all his bufinefs, delight, and
employment, feems to be that of perfe-
cuting Mrs. W——. In the courfe of
laft fummer he arrefted her for the pal-
try fum of twenty-five pounds, which,
from the natural confequences of not
paying immediately, amounted to fixty
pounds, and upwards. Indeed, could
the whole conduct of this old r—l be
fummed up, it would be impoffible to
defcribe his cruelty to Mrs. W. which
proceeds merely from his refolution not
to live with a wretch, whofe cruelty,
and her own difpofition, obliges her to
defpife. It is from fuch kind of ufage
as this that has taught Mrs. W. prudence
and

and difcretion in all her engagements
with the men, nor will fhe ever admit a
vifitor to take any liberties, without firft
knowing the value he fits on her company; and from the appearance which
her prefent keeper enables her to make,
fhe expects to be fomething confiderable.

Mrs. Sp—nc—r, No. 35, *Newman-*
Street, Oxford-Road.

Wine whets the wit, improves its native force,
And gives a pleafant flavour to difcourfe.

This is fully verified in Mrs. S. who
is never fo good a companion as when a
little enlivened with the juice of the grape,
but, always guided by prudence and difcretion, fhe never goes fo far as to render
herfelf the leaft unpleafant. Her figure
is tall, elegant, and ftately.

Her full orb'd cheft lie open to the gale,
And teach the lily whitenefs in the vale.

Her legs and feet are particularly neat
and clean; fhe fings a good fong, is a
very good friend to mirth and good humour, and always fteers clear of vulga-

L   rity.

rity. She is now in her twentieth year, poffeffed of every charm that encouraging age can boaft, and but a very few months has left Hampfhire; we therefore think two guineas beftowed upon her cannot be regretted.

Mifs C—rb—t, No. 16, *Goodge-ftreet*.

Panting fhe lay, and fetch'd long double fighs,
Whilft with thick mifts pleafure had dimm'd
    her eyes.

Some girls have been debauched by delufive arts, and under promifes of marriage, and others have commenced harlots through want, but neither of thefe motives actuated this lady's principles; it was mere lewdnefs that overpowered all nature's works, and ftamped the principles of conjunction and copulation at a very early period: Ere twelve fummers had warmed her conftitution, fhe learned the ufe of different machines, and felt the effects of friction as foon as fhe had any genial fluid within her. Who firft ftamped her virgin mould, we are at a lofs to tell, but from the luxuriance of
the

the prefent foil, guefs it was broke open
at an early period. She is a very lufcious
looking piece, with dark eyes and hair, a
very good complexion, tall, and genteely
formed, with a charming flender leg, and
a pretty foot, which fhe never troubles
the gentlemen to ftoop very low to have
a perfect view of. She is very good natured, fings a good fong, and is in bed a
charming companion, particularly at this
feafon of the year;   for fhe is defirous of
having every part in contact the whole
night. In regard to price, fhe has one
fixed rule ; fhe always meafures a gentleman's *may-pole* by a ftandard of *nine
inches*, and expects a guinea for every
inch it is fhort of full meafure.

Mifs G—rd—ner, No. 47, *Union-ftreet,
Oxford ftreet.*

She thruft among the bufhes her fair hand,

To draw the plant ; and every plant fhe drew,

She fhook the ftalk, and brufh'd away the dew.

This lady's character anfwers exceedingly well to her name, being exquifitely
well fkilled in the art of *raifing* plants in
a *hct-bed*; this fhe practices on her own
bottom,

bottom, but ftill wifhes for a *partner* to be concerned in the bufinefs. Her perfon is pleafing, fhe has the *rofes* in her cheeks, encircled with beds of never fading *lilys*; is as ftrait as a pine of two years growth, though not quite fo tall; her locks fhine like black maiden hair, and fhe is as full of juice as *a ripe amber goofe-berry*; fhe takes a guinea to be *engrafted* upon, and is a very agreeable fprig of *hare-hound*. She is much efteemed by the lovers of *planting*, for having a beautiful fhow of *navel wcrt*, and her fondnefs for *rampions* and *amber vitæ*, fhe defpifes *fool-ftones*, *cuckow pintle*, *Jews ears*, or *birch*; but particularly likes *Adam's Apple-tree*, *fenfitive plant*, *ftich-wort*, *nutmegs*, and fuch valuable productions. To all fuch fhe is free, for her *lips* opens her *lady's mantle*, enclofes them in her *convolvulus*, pours down a whole volley of *feed*, and never quits them whilft they have a *drop* of *fap*.

Mifs Louifa M-nf-n, No. 12, *Wells-ftreet*.

What various charms can M-nf-n boaft,
 By nature thus befriended ;
Whofe legs impart a charm when crofs'd,
 And charming when extended.

Obferve her well, the oblique glance, the lafcivious look, the frequent heave of
 the

the breasts fully speak her inward feelings ; but can any of our readers account for her immoderate fondness for sugar plumbs ? it must certainly be that that induced her to take the famous little Jemmy B—tl—r into her train, the *upper mouth* he keeps constantly supplied with its favourite food ; but we fear *Jemmy* has not parts sufficient to supply the *lower* with a tenth part of *its* necessary food. She therefore solicits the favours of the good natured public for the necessary supplies to that inchanting spot. She is of a good size, and every limb well proportioned. Knowing the beauty of her hand and arm, she takes particular care they shall not pass unnoticed for want of being seen; convinced, of the delicate proportion of her leg and foot, she is very careful their covering shall not discredit them, and has a pleasing knack of keeping them constantly exposed to sight ; and being taught by the eyes of her admirers the influence her neck and breasts command, she covers them with so thin a veil, that the smallest blue branch is easily discovered ; her eyes she cannot hide, nor does she wish it ; they are plain indications

of

of nature's central ſpot, and beam with all the fire of the *enchanting ſpot*. Two guineas is her price, and ſhould Jemmy be there he muſt retire if ſhe thinks fit.

———————

Mrs. Antr—b—s, No. 8, *Liſle-ſtreet, Leiceſter-Fields*.

————..What woman, when
Her blood boils up, and wantons in her veins,
When her hot panting pulſe beats to the joy ;
What woman then would quench her generous
    flame
In an inactive tedious huſband's arms,
That fires and jades our expectation
In the firſt ſtretch of love ; then duly falls
To his old trot, and drudges out the courſe?

Altho' we cannot aſſert that this lady is actually married, we can with truth venture to affirm there are many that have entered the matrimonial circle, that does not poſſeſs the ſame degree of conſtancy for their huſbands, as this lady does for her generous keeper. He is to be ſure an Hibernian gentleman and a captain, two powerful inducements, or rather compellers, to her keeping
within

within bounds ; the firft being generally
paffionate and cruel when irritated, and
the profeffion of the latter is, we muft
imagine, a powerful bar. But ftill fhe is
not impregnable, and where a gentleman (for that he muft be) poffeffes the
proper means, there is not much doubt
of his fuccefs ; flattery is a bait that few
females can withftand, let every word
and action be well cloathed in her
richeft garb ; this incenfe muft be offer'd at the fhrine with pains, perfeverance,
honour, fecrecy, and liberality joined with it, and when fhe is thoroughly
convinced that you poffefs all thefe requifites, fhe will unfold her *haven* of
delight, and put you in poffeffion of
fuch charms that would not difgrace a
monarch's couch ; her tell-tale lafcivious
eye acts as a charming index to that un-
quenchable flame that fills the whole
frame, and fwallows up the other fenfes ;
fhe is rather fhort, but admirably well
made, and when once convinced of the
honour and parts of her paramour, gives
fuch a loofe to her unbounded appetite,
that very few of the Cyprian choir can
match her.

Mifs

Mifs H—ll—n, No. 2, *Glanville-ftreet.*

Oh fhe is all the heart would wifh, or eye admire,
The pureft child of love by beauty fir'd ;
Whom but to love, need only but to fee,
To fee, admire, fuch heaven born fymmetry ;
To touch, to feel, ah, there's the potent hold
That chains the will, and molds the fnowy heart
To love's delightful glow ; the milky hills
Half rifing, half fuppreff'd, with glowing ardor
Afk corporeal preffure, and invite
The *carnal weapon* to its burning fheath.

This lady, in confequence of a trivial
fall out with her parents, (which by the
bye fhe had long fought for)left her home,
and flufhed with all the fire of youth
impetuous ; burning with every defire
the young hand of luft could create, and
ftill a ftranger, except in idea, to the
grand *fubduer* of their fires, fhe fought
this expanded field of delight, nor fought
in vain ; her youth and perfon foon
attracted the eye of an old male veteran
in our band, and her innocence and
fimplicity were foon overpowered, her
maiden honours plucked, and all her
virgin claims at once lie dead. The
lively girl in queftion is now entering
her fixteenth year, has only been four
months

months on the town, the thinly *covered* grot below has therefore not yet fufficiently felt the general influence of its much fought for *acquaintance,* to be very thickly covered, ftill fhe thinks it proof againft any attack, nor fears to meet the moft vigorous, tho' deftitute of every other weapon. She is rather darkly complexioned, with fine hazel eyes, is fhort, and inclinable to be lufty, and as pretty a leg and foot as man would with to divide, which any good natured man, with two guineas in his pocket that he has no objection to fpare, may lie between the whole livelong night, and tafte all the raptures he can poffibly expect to meet with, in one as yet fo untutored in the art.

Madam D—fl—z, No. 46, *Frith-ftreet,*
        Soho.

   Si javois pour heritage,
      Le trefor le plus charmant,
   Je vous en donnerois en gage,
      Et mon cœur pour un prefent.

It is only fix months that this lady has left her native country, and at prefent
                        fpeaks

fpeaks very little Englifh. She is young
and lively, (but ftill does not feem to
poffefs fo much vivacity as the majority
of her countrywomen ;) fhe loves to
revenge her countrymen's caufe on the
Englifh, by doing what the moft valor-
ous Frenchman would never effect, that
is, to bring Britons on their knees ; fhe
is now about twenty-two, rather fhort
and fat, with a plump face, and fuch a
roguifh lear in her eye, that cannot be
refifted. Several of our brave officers
have fpent fome of their *beft blood* in her
fervice, and regretted they had no more
to *fhed.* Her lovely dark hair feems like
a net to catch lovers, and her lower tendrils, which fport on her alabafter mount
of Venus, are formed to give delight. She
has one qualification which many Englifh
girls want, which is a certain cleanlinefs
in the Netherlands. They are contented
to wafh their faces, necks, and hands ;
but Mademoifelle, like many of her
countrywomen, thinks that not enough ;
fhe performs conftant ablutions on the
gulph of pleafure, and keeps it conftantly
frefh, cool, and clean, never putting
a morfel into that mouth, till fhe has
fully abfterged every poffible remnant of
the laft meal. She conftantly mounts
her

her *bidet*, and with a large fponge laves the whole extent of the parifh of the mother of all faints. Some may, perhaps, think her a female fpy, or a fmuggler ; but furely a girl, who fo freely difclofes her own fecrets, can have no improper aim at thofe of government ; and her commodity cannot be pronounced as contraband when it hath fo often been duly entered.

She dreffes quite in the French ftile and tafte, lays on a profufion of rouge and pearl powder, and is not particularly partial to money, but will condefcend to take a couple of guineas, *not as payment, but folely as, 'une gage d'amour.*

Mifs Emma Ell——tt, No. 8, *Afton- ftreet, Gray's-Inn-Lane.*

Our fouls their former joys renew,
  We raife new fport, and wanton jefting ;
  Our eyes eachothers charms review,
  In every form of love contefting.
At laft, our body's warm'd with mutual
  fire,
To prove each others aid to join in one
  confpire.

This truly lovely woman is about twenty, and, whilft fhe remains in a
ftate

ftate of filence, commands every attracting charm the heart of man can wifh;
fhe fpeaks French tolerably well, and
fings inimitably; fhe has now trod the
path of love four years, during which
time pretty Emma has experienced every
viciffitude the cruel hand of fortune could
poffibly inflict. At prefent Mr. B. a
merchant, in Caftle-Court, is the gentleman from whom fhe derives her principal fupport; fhe has fine blue melting
eyes, with an aquiline nofe, and a very
pretty mouth, when her tongue is inactive, but when once fhe gives a loofe
to that unruly member, fhe pours forth
fuch a torrent of blackguardifm that fhall
deftroy every attracting feature, and
fpoil one of the moft defirable looking
girls in the *Cyprian market.* Our damfel
is therefore the moft agreeable looking
girl when afleep; in bed fhe is truly
amorous, and a charming fportfwoman,
and when one ftrain is finifhed, cries, *da
capo*, with a good grace, for which fhe
expects five guineas.

Mifs

Mis T—s—n, No. 2, *Glanville-Street.*

Had love's fair goddefs been fo ftrong in charms,
Rafh Diomede had dropt his vent'rous arms ;
No fhameful victory the Greek had won,
But had a thoufand wounds receiv'd inftead of
    giving one.

This tit bit is not above fixteen, rather fhort, but pretty, having an excellent complexion, with fine blue eyes, light hair, and a very white, and regular fet of teeth. Altho' fhe has not been fix months upon the *Pave de Londres,* (having received a complete education, has learnt to dance, fpeak French, and play upon the guittar; and has likewife been initiated into all the myfteries of the Cyprian fchool; having read *les Bejoux Indifcrets*; the *Woman of Pleafure*; Rochefter's Poems ;) fhe is *au fait de tout.* Add to this, fhe has often viewed with rapture all *Aretin's* poftures, and longed for the practice, as well as the theory. No wonder then that fhe fhould be inclined to give delight in every poffible attitude, and has no kind of objection to yield, with becoming modefty, to take a *coup* à la *levrette.* She is at prefent in keeping by a citizen, who has fuffered

M

her

her to affume his name, but is always
pleafed when Mr. T. is not with her, to
accommodate any gentleman in her *pretty apartment* a whole night, for which
fhe expects two guineas.

Mifs Harriet B—r—n, No. 8, *Taviftock-row.*

In framing thee, heav'n took unufual care,
And ftampt thee faireft of the *Cretan* fair.

There is fomething fo very engaging
in the perfon of this lady, that thofe gentlemen, who once vifit her, feldom or
ever fail repeating it. In her deportment
fhe is free and open, without the leaft
tinge of affectation, in fize rather below
mediocrity, fine dark hair, and bewitching black eyes; a complexion between
the fair and brunette: her features are
remarkably delicate, and, conjunctively
taken, fully verifies the Poet.

None can obferve her features but approve,
There's grace with beauty, dignity with love.

Her breafts are finely proportioned, and
delicately moulded for love's tender attack,
and fwell and recede the melting language

guage of the heart; the grave beneath,
delicately fhaded by a *fable thicket*, is
fraught with all its proper fenfibility,
and. well knowing the value of her charms,
fhe is not one that can be fported with,
nor will fhe fuffer any liberty beyond the
ftricteft bounds of decency to take place,
without the payment of one piece before
hand.

Mifs W—ll—ms,   No. 3,   *Glanville-
·ftreet.*

Firm breafts, white belly, and fuch thighs,
Gaze ghaftly envy, and forget her fize.

This lady's affable temper, and engaging difpofition, fully compenfates
for her fize, which is rather diminutive,
and the innumerable beauties of her face;
when put in competition with this deficiency, ought entirely to efface the fmall-
eft idea of it. From her youth we might
be led to imagine her deficient in the
practice of love, but we can affure our
readers he will meet but few in the *cyprian field* that will fhew better fport;
her hair is a beautiful gloffy dark brown;
her eye brows finely arch'd, and of the

M 2   fame

fame hue, which, contrasted by a pair of beautiful cerulean eyes, and cheeks of living roses and lilies, places her in the rank of first rate beauties,

> Her rising breasts two hillocks are of snow,
> On which two little fragrant rose buds grow;

below which descends the smooth tract of a belly, which conveys to the mind an idea of animated ivory, at the bottom of which is display'd a lovely chesnut fringe, terminated by a pouting *flash hole*, which is far from being insensible to the raptures of its *grisly antagonist*, and with pleasure *opens* its *mouth* to receive his well erected crest, who *enters* with his accustomed pride, but soon returns with *fallen head*, as if conscious of its presumption; but the *mistress* of this formidable *enemy* is well acquainted with the means of restoring life to the *vanquished member*, but only to make it more sensible of its inability. Mercenary views are far from what she aims at; she can give and receive a *luscious* share of the pleasures of *copulation*; but beginning to know the accustom'd ways of the baser sort of men, and not being always confident of the honour of her *paramour*, if he is a

stranger,

ftranger, fhe muft receive her compliment of half a guinea, or a guinea, according to the length of the intended
vifit, before fhe proceeds to any kind of
bufinefs.

Mifs Fanny H—nl—y, No 14, *King-
ftreet, Saint James's Square.*

Her every thought, and wifhes, and defires,
Agree with yours, and burn with mutual fires.

This merry little lively tit appears to
be about fixteen, and is never to be met
without a fmile upon her countenance,
and a frifky fong at her tongue's end ;
fhe is very fhort, a brunette in complexion, with a luftfully fparkling eye,
and jetty ringlets down her back. The fifter hills, with their bewitching coral
pinnacles, are irreftibly firm, and fpeak
their filent language very forcibly to the
heart. The grove beneath, fhading the
font of life, is dreft in fable, and fe-
cures the *internal manfion* from any fudden *attack*. She is generally very expe-
ditious in dying, therefore we would advife her antagonift to pufh the warm con-
M 3   teft

eft with agility, or it will not be a *dead*
heat; fhe is a very willing and amorous
bedfellow, never againft repetition, and
fuch a good naturd, and good temper'd creature, that fhe feems to fay to
every one,

With thee fecur'd,—I'd fmile at fortune's
· frowns,
And all her threats defy,—nor court her
fmiles.

Mifs Jenny K—b—rd, No. 33, *Nor-
thumberland-ftreet, Strand.*

You gaulky fteeple, you ftalking ftag,
Your hufband muft come, from Brobdignag,

It is a pity that fo noble a piece could
not be preferved folely for the ufe of his
Majefty's Grenadiers ; fhe is more than
fix foot; fhe is now about twenty-five,
poffeffes an elegance in her perfon, (we
wifh we could pay the fame compliment
to her actions) light hair and eyes, which
are continually lighted up by the all powerful brandy bottle ; as fhe excells in the
height of ftature fo is fhe the height of
good nature, for fhe never refufes any
gentleman

(139)

gentleman her favors, that has any money in his pocket; she is surely too the height of vulgarity, for she will come her *eyes and limbs,* with any lady from Billingsgate, or Jack tar from Wapping; but her greatest fault, and what makes more disgusting her other imperfections, is her violent attachment to drinking; she generally contrives to pin her basket completely by nine o'clock; then she swears most abominably, and is as great a proficient in barefaced indecency, as Messalina of antient Rome. We therefore set her up as a beacon; in spite of all, when she pleases, she can be a good companion, and speaks the English language remarkably well; she is never denied to any one, except Mr. G. a watchmaker, in the city, should be engaged with her, he being her particular friend.

Mrs. Charlotte F—ne, No. 41, *King Street, Soho.*

To tell the beautie's of the place,
 How weak is human tongue;
The noble fringes which it grace,
 In golden ringlets hung.

Charlotte received a good education, and was once far above the perambulating

lating clafs of nymphs, and might, perhaps, have remained fo, had not her
violent attachment to the curs'd buckle
and belt fociety, rendered her difgufting
in the eyes of all her friends; Mr.
G—bl—t, brother to a tallow chandler,
of Carnaby-Market, took particular notice of her, and removed her once from
her hated crew, allowed her a tolerable
provifion, and would have continued
her friend, had not her rage for the old
fociety made him forfeit his efteem. She
is now rather in the wane, having feen
at leaft twenty-eight fummers, tall, and
very well proportioned ; her complexion
is but indifferent, but, being a native of
Germany, is not to be wondered at ; fhe
fpeaks French alfo, but we cannot get
her to confefs fhe has been ten years on
the town, unlefs you pay her a *guinea fee*
for confefling.

Mrs. W—tp—l, No. 2, *Poland-Street,*
Oxford-Street.

She'fmil'd, and gave a kifs might Jove difarm,
And from his hand the brandifhed thunder
charm.

If this good natured willing girl fhould
chance to be engaged herfelf, fhe will
with

with the greateſt pleaſure provide her
gentleman with another companion;
ſhe is a genteel woman, and a very
chearful companion, completely miſtreſs of the ſport, and can *turn* and
twiſt in all the enchanting folds of love,
and preſs you to her breaſt,

In all the extatic raptures of a lover ;

will enjoy, or ſeem to enjoy, every *high
toned* ſenſation; will bend eagerly to
meet the *ſucculent ſhower* of bliſs, and
repeat the amorous conteſt as frequently
as you pleaſe, being firſt *convinced* that
you will make her a guinea richer in the
morning.

Mrs. Gr—ff—n, *near Union-Stairs, Wapping.*

This is a comely woman, about forty,
and boaſts ſhe can give more pleaſure
than a dozen raw girls. Indeed ſhe has
acquired great experience, in the courſe
of twenty years ſtudy, in *natural philoſophy*,
in the univerſity of Portſmouth, where
ſhe was long the ornament of the back
of the point. She is perfectly miſtreſs
of

of all her actions, and can proceed re-
gularly from the dart of her tongue, and
the soft tickle of her hand, to the extatic squeeze of her thighs; the enchanting
twine of her legs; the elaborate suction
of her lower lips, and the melting flood
of delight, with which she constantly
bedews the *moffy root* of the tree of *life*,
and washes the testimonies of manhood; tho' past her meridian, she is
still agreeable; her eyes are black as
well as her hair, of which she has an
abundance both above and below, her
breasts are large but not flabby, and her
skin is fair. Five shillings is her price,
and she earns it with great industry: but
if her lover seems capable of prolonging
the *delicious banquet*, and is remarkably
well provided, she will abate *weight* for
inches. Her chief and best customers
are sea officers, whom she particularly
likes, as they do not stay long at home,
and always return fraught with love and
presents.

Mademoiselle

Madamoifelle Du Par, No. 19, *Carlifle-
ftreet, Soho.*

Dieux ; qu'a t-il vu, que d'appas enchanteurs !
Sous un bofquet, d'ou coule une fountaine,
Ou chaque mois le doux printemps ramene ;
Pour nos plaifirs, l'abondance & les fleurs,
It voit un trou, le joli precipice ;
Ce n'etaci point le trou de faint Patrice.

This lady has lately been a teacher in a
French boarding fchool, but taking a liking to a young Clergyman in the neighbourhood, fhe made a conjunction of
calvanifm with the eftablifhed church,
and he propagated the gofpel in her *foreign parts* with great affiduity ; but her
immoderate love of the fport, after
having once tafted the power of the *Bri-
tifh conftitution,* fpeedily brought her to
our market, here to her great difcredit
and lofs fhe has form'd a connection
with a boy by the name of N—wb—y,
brother to the noted attorney well known
as a flafh man among the ladies, and one
whofe principles will not bear the ftricteft
fcrutiny. She is a tall, genteel looking
figure,

figure, ſpeaks Engliſh pretty'well, fine
dark eyes and hair, a tolerable complexion, thanks to Mr. Warren, who oc-
caſionally fills up thoſe indentions the
ſmall pox has been buſy in making, and
makes her a deſirable piece enough.
Her low countries are ſaid to be of ample dimenſions, and ſhe is ſo publick ſpir-
ited, that ſhe makes no diſtinction of
perſons or nations; but will ſay, *je vous
remercie*, to any man for the ſmalleſt
piece of gold.

Miſs W—rn—r, at Mrs. Wood's, *Liſle-Street, Leiceſter-Fields.*

Embrace me cloſe, and join thy lips to mine,
There's no ſecurity in other joys;
Here happineſs is rivetted alone;
Here nothing fades, nothing decays, the ſweets
Immortal are, and never ceaſe to ſpring.

This is a fine girl, lately come from
Cambridge, and juſt dancing into her
twentieth year, we have known her but
a very little time, but from her complexion, which is bordering on the
brunette,

brunette; her lively hazel eyes, and
the lovely pouting orbs of nature, we can
venture to affirm her no bad sportswoman;
the *grove beneath* is beautifully border'd
by a *sable fringe*, the *ruby portals* of
which when unfolded, display the *coral
tipt janitor* strutting in all the luscious
mess of full fraught womanhood, and
will safely-conduct the well erected engine
into the harbour of delight, and bath
him, in the choicest sweets of nature, for
two pounds, two shillings.

WE muſt now bid adieu to our courteous reader, and wiſh him every ſucceſs
that youth, health, love, and wine can
poſſibly inſpire him with ; hoping, at the
ſame time, that they will throw a friendly
veil over all the unavoidable errors that
may have happen'd in this work, and
excuſe that diſagreeable tautology, which,
for want of other words, we are neceſſitated to make, and not to be diſpleas'd if
they find the ſame ladies in this liſt that
appear'd before in other names ; for, as
their reſidence is chang'd as often as their
names, it is almoſt impoſſible but ſome
ſuch miſtakes muſt happen ; and hope
that the attention that is now paid to the
procuring the beſt and moſt reſpectable,
will wipe off every other blot.

We likewiſe take leave of the ladies,
and are particularly happy to think that
what was formerly ſeen in the eyes of
our world a diſgrace, is now conſidered
pleaſing, delightful, and honourable.

F I N I S.

www.ingramcontent.com/pod-product-compliance
Lightning Source LLC
Chambersburg PA
CBHW020506270326
41926CB00008B/766